GOD'S WAY WITH MAN

There is in God, some say,
A deep but dazzling darkness, as men here
Say it is late and dusky, because they
                See not all clear;
    Oh, for that night, where I in him
    Might live invisible and dim!

HENRY VAUGHAN

GOD'S WAY WITH MAN

Variations on the Theme of Providence

Roger Hazelton

NEW YORK   ABINGDON PRESS   NASHVILLE

GOD'S WAY WITH MAN

Copyright © MCMLVI by Abingdon Press

Library of Congress Catalog Card Number: 56-10146

SET UP, PRINTED, AND BOUND BY THE
PARTHENON PRESS, AT NASHVILLE,
TENNESSEE, UNITED STATES OF AMERICA

PREFACE

Although this book deals with some momentous issues, it is actually a rather modest approach to them. It has grown slowly, but inescapably, out of my conviction that the doctrine of God's providence has not received from present-day theologians the attention it deserves. True, my chosen theme has doubtless lost for many if not most of us the naturalness and lived reality it used to have. Its affirmations have become questions. Is God in actual control of human destiny? Does he take anything like a personal interest in the course of events? Can he be counted on to support and undergird our striving after good in the face of so much that is plainly evil in the world we have to live in? Today many people start out with a prejudice against the very notion of providence. They are likely to agree with one of the characters in a play by Christopher Fry that

> A man has to provide his own providence,
> Or there's no knowing what religion will get hold of him.[1]

Thus it is that this great doctrine, which lies so near the heart of Christian worship, preaching, and pastoral work, has not yet come as it should into the focus of our theological task. And this is something of a pity, for while theologians have been notably busy elsewhere, our popular religiousness as expressed in jazzed-up

[1] From *The Dark Is Light Enough*. Used by permission of Oxford University Press, Inc.

5

lyrics, televised dramatics, or radio counseling has become practically saturated with a notion of Providence as crude as it is
curious. I believe, therefore, that theologians owe their fellow
Christians something better and truer than they have been getting.

But how shall we proceed? We might treat Providence in
time-honored systematic fashion, developing it into a comprehensive unity of thought and relating it carefully to other doctrines of
our faith. In this book no such effort will be found. That is mainly
because I do not think that such an approach makes real contact
with the folk who most need to be reached. If we are going to
reconstitute the idiom and the idea of Providence in our time,
we must first of all identify ourselves with them in those very
situations of lostness, dread, or emptiness where the thought of a
guiding, guarding, governing God is being sharply questioned.

We do this best in Christian theology by coming at the doctrine of providence not systematically but strategically, by trying
to see God at work in just those experiences from which he
seems to be evacuated. We must, I think, permit our belief to
shine through the darkness of our doubt. That is, in fact, the
genius of this particular doctrine.

And so I have conceived this book as a group of variations on
the providential theme, modeled frankly on a musical and not
the usual architectural pattern. There is a recurrent theme, given
out in various contexts and with different accents. Hence no
single chapter stands alone, nor is it to be thought of as a definitive answer to the issues which it evokes. Yet each, I hope, is a
genuine thread within the living web of thought which makes
up the whole doctrine. If the chapters seem to overlap one another, and they do, that is because a common theme is running
through them all. Some are in minor, others in predominantly
major, key. And what they leave us with is not some logically
constructed edifice of thought but rather a fabric of conviction,

not too tightly woven to be true and yet not too loosely put together to be false. A pattern borrowed from music seems the best way to convey the substance of this doctrine of God's sovereign concern for man.

Another bit of self-explaining may be in order here. Some readers may get discouraged by the large amount of attention given to so-called *avant-garde* writers and thinkers. In my defense I can only say that a Christian conversation with them is already long overdue, for it is they who pose the questions about Providence in the most unavoidable way. At the same time I feel quite sure that the argument of the book can be followed by many who are not yet acquainted with these writers, although their work cannot long be disregarded by anyone who wishes to think seriously and searchingly about Providence in our own day.

There remains the pleasant and grateful task of acknowledging some occasions which prodded the book into being. The Alden-Tuthill Lectures at the Chicago Theological Seminary in 1953 first gave me the chance to get my thoughts into communicable shape. An invitation to deliver the Taylor Lectures at Yale University in 1955 enabled me to expand and deepen my work on the chosen theme; and these were repeated as the annual spring lectures to the clergy of Washington, D.C., the same year. Portions of Chapters Five and Eight are drawn from articles which have appeared in the *Journal of Religion* and the *International Journal of Religious Education*. I am happy to have so many good friends to thank for the encouragement that has resulted in this book. I want to add a special word of appreciation to my students at Andover Newton Theological School, who have done more than they will ever know to sharpen my thinking and, I may gratefully add, to strengthen my believing.

ROGER HAZELTON

CONTENTS

1

The Question About Destiny

Our theme in this book is an august and venerable one—the meaning of God's providence as it is bound up with the tangled, often obscure destinies of men and women living in the world. It is the sort of theme which stretches the mind and probes the heart. It leads us into a realm where even the most venturesome and independent thinkers hesitate to tread. Entering it, we soon abandon the palpable securities of everyday experience in exchange for the more rugged terrain of reality itself. Here familiar landmarks are few, and fewer still are guarantees of safe arrival. Instead there is the peril of exposure to the very elements of existence, sheer yet beckoning in their immensity.

But this same theme has very much to do with the common scenes of daily life. It is here, if anywhere, that God's voice must be heard, his will declared, his ways revealed. In one sense Providence is the homeliest of all our Christian doctrines, as it deals so plainly with men and women in the very midst of their ongoing life. It is in those things we know best—our personal choices, meetings with one another, and all manner of delights and duties—that we have to detect and piece out whatever thread of meaning or of purpose is vouchsafed to us. Yes, to speak of destiny and Providence is to speak of that intricate web of life in which we all are most at home.

May there not then be something paradoxical about this theme? How shall we hold what is so intimately ours in close relationship with what is ultimately God's? At all events we have to try, since that is exactly the burden of thought and faith which such a theme imposes. To think rigorously and to believe heartily, and both at once, is what this subject clearly demands. A very large part of what the providence of God means is involved in this attempt to maintain the conviction that God is working and willing, in and through the passing events that make up what we call the world. For this doctrine brings significantly into view the ultimate import of intimately known things.

I

But it is of human destiny that I must speak first. Concern with destiny has always been, and doubtless will remain, a trait that is uniquely human. There may have been more placid, self-assured times than our own when destiny was not so much in the front and center of our thought. Perhaps then it was more a matter of simple curiosity, this question about destiny, as if the careful winnowing of historical data or the searching of the Scriptures could yield the kernel of an answer. However, that is not our situation now. This question clings tenaciously and insidiously to everything we do or have or are or wish to be. Among us destiny is questioned by men and women who have lost their way in being and greatly yearn to find it again.

Agnostics will declare the question to be quite unanswerable, and dogmatists will answer it too eagerly and abruptly; but there are surely few in our day who would regard it as altogether pointless or fruitless. The great majority of us live in the middle zone between these two extremes, and are inescapably concerned with the whence and whither of our living. This questioning, moreover, also discloses much about the questioner himself. Almost by definition man is the being who asks questions, and his questions get their very shape and impetus from man's own image of himself. In fact, they frame a kind of self-portrait of man himself. Although I may be altogether incapable of confidently putting into words exactly who I am, my style of life consists in wrestling with the question about destiny and makes its own implicit reply to it.

One does not need to be listening to a lecture on the philosophy of history in order to become alerted to this incessant, throbbing question, but may merely be looking through the daily paper before breakfast. The latest airplane crash or the current diplomatic impasse may be quite enough to rouse the question from the depths to which it has perhaps been long repressed. It is posed most obviously and summarily by large-scale happenings within the social and natural orders; but it also has a way of coming to the fore through the agency of less dramatic, middle-sized events, or even apparently inconsequential ones—those tricks and turns of life that steal upon us and catch us unawares. More often than not, it is this jarring of routine, this jolting out of what is taken pretty much for granted, that evokes a deep perplexity regarding the bent and bearing of happenings in which we find ourselves involved.

But though such happenings, whether trivial or great, serve to put the question about destiny, they are not able to silence it. That is because they do not and cannot generate out of themselves a simple answer which satisfies the questioner. No enumerating and classifying of events, not even the historian's effort to group them into massive trends and movements, can fulfill so deep a need. If past occurrences do not lend themselves to the purpose of confident generalization, what shall be said of those that constitute the present or contemporaneous world? Like man himself, they are pregnant with paradox and baffling in their strangeness.

At the same time it must be kept in mind that no fact is a

bare fact and no event a mere event. To be sure, we sometimes speak and act as if this were the case; but our so-called objectivity is really nothing more or less than deliberate self-isolation. Often, indeed, this is a necessary and worthy undertaking; by means of it, for example, science wins its theoretical and practical victories; but it is nonetheless important that we should recognize what we are doing when we construct the picture of a world in which man is a kind of perpetual stranger. G. K. Chesterton wrote somewhere that every morning God says to the sun, "Get up!" Most of us would probably not go so far as to believe this. But certainly we must agree that sunrise means not simply an event transpiring out in neutral nature; its connection with human work and purpose is neither adventitious nor imagined, but is genuinely bound up with its very occurrence. Hence what any happening *means* is part and parcel of what it *is*.

This of course must not become an excuse for wanting to impose upon events those meanings of our own to which they are expected to conform. Incidentally, this has been the besetting sin of many crude and wooden forms of the doctrine of Providence. They have been expressions not of mankind's natural piety but of a stubborn, optimistic practicality. This sort of premature providentialism is almost always the result of human impatience, not of real faith. To live with destiny, as we shall soon see, is to live with mystery. Yet the actual form which any question about destiny takes is one concerning neither events alone, nor meaning alone, but what we may call the meaning of events or the eventfulness of meaning. When the Hebrew prophets and psalmists discerned God's almighty hand at work in growing grain and thunderstorms, in battles and the birth of children, they were not so much guilty of reading into events the meaning which they wanted to find there as they were intent upon discovering within their very texture and momentum an inner and controlling power. But this is to anticipate; the point to be made now is that it is here in this eventful world that what is meaningful belongs and is to be discovered.

If the question is put in any other way, then destiny stands mute. It will not yield up its secrets to either the purely inquisitive or the overly insistent mind. My questioning, after all, must be relevant—not simply to my own desires and plans, but to the whole order of existence to which the question itself is addressed. Thus while it goes well beyond mere curiosity, it must fall far short of doctrinaire assurance. Such a questioning launches me out upon a voyage of discovery in which I must be prepared to be surprised quite as much as satisfied. Actually what I am doing is to try out for size, as it were, my principle of meaningful interpretation upon the world in which I also belong. I may not avow this principle openly; I may indeed take considerable pains to disguise it; and yet sooner or later it will be disclosed for what it is. When this happens, it may come with disturbing self-revelation to him who—in Cardinal Newman's words—has such a principle as his reason without being able to give it as his reason.

In asking our questions about destiny, then, we are actually disclosing what it means to be a questioner, not merely seeking some conformity between our own supposedly subjective wishes and an equally hypothetical objective order. Let us go even further: Can anyone possibly ask such a question without also giving some hint of the answer which he is ready to entertain? Without of course implying that the question answers itself, we must nevertheless say that it is always directed toward a power of being competent to give the answer. Otherwise it is not the question about destiny at all, but a sort of general wonderment flung out against a nonresponsive vacuum. And even this is to give an answer prematurely. What I have in mind can be indicated by a brief passage from Søren Kierkegaard, a way of putting this question which has become classic: "Who am I? How came I here? What is this thing called the world? . . . Why was I not consulted? . . . How did I obtain an interest in this big enterprise they call reality? . . . And if I am to be compelled to take part in it, where is the director? I should like to make a remark to him." [1]

Plainly Kierkegaard was a man of strong faith, although here he seems to speak with the accent of doubt. And yet his own way of putting the question, just because it finds common ground with unbelief, serves to point up the role of faith in specifying the object of one's doubt. It needs, I think, to be remembered that doubt and faith are not fixed quantities or mutually exclusive states at all, but rather mutually involved and interpenetrating. Thus doubt itself, no matter how deeply rooted, is never simply belieflessness. It is not lack of faith or nonfaith but unfaith. It is what Aldous Huxley —who ought to know—calls a "God-shaped blank"; that is, it has the nature of an aching void. From this it is apparent that doubt can rather easily assume the form of resentment or suspicion against whatever power is held responsible for one's present vote of No Confidence. Thus doubt regarding destiny means calling the powers that be to an accounting.

And this must mean, in turn, that every honest doubt concerning destiny is also strangely a kind of faith in destiny. That faith, to be sure, may yet be mostly negative and rendered in a muted and minor key. But no one asks Kierkegaard's sort of question unless he believes in his own right to raise it, as well as in the possibility of some reply to it. For note that the same "director" to whom Kierkegaard would like to make a remark is exactly the target of his doubt, by whom alone his doubt can be met and resolved. Just what this singular fact means, that despair of destiny bespeaks a certain confidence in destiny, will become clearer as we probe more

---

[1] *Repetition*, tr. Walter Lowrie (Princeton, N. J.: Princeton University Press, 1941), p. 114. Used by permission of the publisher.

nearly to the center of the question itself. Right now, however, let us be content with noting that the question's very form is a significant indication of the answer that is sought, and may even foreshadow the character of that answer.

II

A bit earlier it was said that the question about destiny is a mirroring of man himself. Nothing reveals a person more accurately than what he expects from life or has against it. Indeed, all thinking about destiny makes man a question to himself and ricochets back upon the thinker. To ask about what being means to me is at once to ask what I mean to being, what it means to be myself. One might even say not only that here the questioner becomes his own question but that he is himself questioned. All attempts to deduce what destiny means from bodily constitution, social conditioning, or natural necessity must sooner or later come to grief upon the rock of my mysterious selfhood. Destiny, properly speaking, is selfhood; and selfhood is a great mystery indeed.

This brings us into view of a significant distinction which had better be made now, since it will follow us all through the pages of this book. It is the distinction between a problem and a mystery, on which Gabriel Marcel has written so much. According to this contemporary French philosopher and man of letters, such a distinction is absolutely essential to an understanding of man.

A problem, as the word itself in Greek indicates, is something that is "out there" set in front of me. It is an impediment to my progress, hence an obstacle to be gotten rid of by appropriate thought or action on my part. I can solve my problem by bringing to bear the relevant techniques or methods, such as social engineering, scientific study, or psychotherapy. By being thus defined and reduced, the problem can be removed; then I can proceed on my human way without having to bother about it any longer. A problem, then, is inert, objective, in principle solvable. Some problems, of course, are tougher than others; but their solution is chiefly a matter of knowing how and doing what you know.

But a mystery, says Marcel, is something else again. In the first place it is not external to me; rather, I am internal to it. In the very nature of the case, therefore, I am unable to extricate myself from it for the purpose of tackling it from the outside. No matter how hard I may try to make something external and objective out of mystery, I remain involved and included in it. Thus while a problem, say in mathematics, is *my* problem, that is, something that belongs quite within the scope of my own comprehension and competence (at least in the last analysis), a mystery such as that of human birth or death is never wholly mine. On the contrary, it has a perennial and irreducible strangeness about it, and resists my attempts to define and reduce it to solvable terms. In fact the more strenuously I try to get hold of a mystery in problematic fashion, the more I find myself entangled and implied in it, so that it finally has hold of me instead.

Does this mean that nothing further can be said about mystery or that it cannot in any way be understood? Not at all. A mystery is a great deal more than a dead end of thought, a blank wall or sheer riddle to the mind. It has indeed the curious property of arousing and encouraging our best and sharpest thought. The awareness of mystery does not mark the end of rational exploration, but its very beginning. To live with mystery is rather like entering a deep forest, said Baron von Hügel once, a forest into which the further you penetrate the darker it becomes; yet there is something sheltering and embracing about this darkness as well as merely forbidding. That within which I am harbored and at home cannot be altogether alien to me, unless I try to wrest its secret by force or fail to respect its magnitude and power.

Now let us apply this distinction to the question with which we are confronted in this chapter. Destiny is truly mysterious, not merely problematic. To conceive destiny at all could only be the privilege of one who is open at both ends, so to speak, to that which is indefinitely, and perhaps even infinitely, mysterious. It is, as was said at the beginning, to enter a realm where venturesome yet humble search becomes us. It means to ask, not how we can "master life," but what it is by which we are encompassed, to which we are accountable, from which our succor is expected. Our task is that of locating the mystery of human destiny and calling it by its right name.

Paul Tillich gives us a good starting point in essaying the following definition:

> Our destiny is that out of which our decisions arise; it is the indefinitely broad basis of our centered selfhood; it is the concreteness of our being which makes all our decisions *our* decisions. . . . This refers to body structure, psychic strivings, spiritual character. It includes the communities to which I belong, the past unremembered and remembered, the environment which has shaped me, the world which has made an impact on me. . . . Destiny is not a strange power which determines what shall happen to me. It is myself as given, formed by nature, history, and myself.[2]

Usually we think of destiny in just the way which Tillich here rejects, after the analogy of a determining pressure exerted on us from outside ourselves. That is, we try to isolate it problematically; we want to avoid our responsibility for it. Whenever I say that I am after all what destiny makes me, I conceive of something over against myself which forces me to be myself. In short, I am attempting to identify destiny with fate—a view which will claim our attention a little later. Tillich's description of destiny, on the other hand, has the very real merit of leaving this basic question

[2] *Systematic Theology* (University of Chicago Press, 1951), I, 184-85.

actually open. He wishes to take fully into account those factors of coercive import which lend plausibility to the idea of fate or fortune while refusing at the same time to identify man's destiny with outer determination or external compulsion of whatever sort. Instead, he thinks of destiny as an inward self-determination, granted its sources in nature and history beyond the self.

Shall we say then that for Tillich destiny means simply freedom? That is what we ordinarily have in mind when we talk about inward self-determination. But to do so would be to misunderstand Tillich rather badly. He takes considerable pains to discriminate between the actual exercise of freedom and the basic set of conditions, operating in and through the self, which makes one's actions genuinely free. Like Augustine and Jonathan Edwards before him, Tillich emphasizes not simply the freedom of the self but the selfhood that is freedom, expressed in every instance of personal choice or action.

Does this seem abstruse or overcomplicated? If so, it can be put in plainer language. Destiny means that whatever I do is the expression of what I am and that what I am is in turn grounded in something far greater than myself. If I prefer poetry to pinochle or write books instead of growing crops, then that is just the kind of person I am. But to be myself is not to be only myself; it means that being has expressed itself in me. This way of thinking makes destiny neither simply freedom nor simply fate, but rather selfhood, or what Tillich calls the "centered totality" of one's being. When I inquire with Kierkegaard, "Who am I?" I am not asking what my name is, where I live, who my parents are, to what country or century I belong. Presumably I know these things already, and certainly none of them are unimportant. But here a kind of question is raised which no amount of itemized knowledge can possibly answer. I am asking of myself what it means to be, what my reason for being really is.

It is possible to make some minor criticisms of this rendering of destiny in terms of selfhood. Tillich does not here suggest what is certainly true, that destiny concerns my future quite as much as my past. And he appears to conceive destiny in a somewhat too individualistic fashion, so that there are as many destinies as there are human selves. Yet this is a conception which is surely sound at the core. Whoever raises the question about destiny does so as a man, not as one among other men only but as a human being in the generic sense. And if he does not ask this question in his own person as an essay in self-understanding, it is no genuine question at all.

We can see this still more clearly if we consider the following fragment from Pascal, to which the passage quoted earlier from Kierkegaard bears a striking resemblance:

> When I consider the short duration of my life, swallowed up in the eternity before and after, the little space which I fill, and even can see, engulfed in the infinite immensity of spaces of which I am ignorant, and which know me not, I am frightened, and am astonished at being here rather than there; for there is no reason why here rather than there, why now rather than then. Who has put me here? By whose order and direction have this place and time been allotted to me?[3]

In its Pascalian form the question about destiny is not so much private as personal, not egocentric so much as existential. The "I" who speaks here is a representative, vicarious self whose question can be repeated indefinitely without losing any of its point and urgency. Such a question must be put not by Olympians but by mortals. It could scarcely have occurred to God, since after all it is a question concerning him. The fact that man asks questions about himself is one of the surest marks of his separation from God. But

[3] Blaise Pascal, *Pensées* (New York: Modern Library, Inc., 1941), pp. 74-75. Used by permission of Random House, Inc.

insofar as the question about destiny is that of any man, it becomes that of everyman, hence also my own. Even more tellingly than Kierkegaard, Pascal wields a poetic and evocative gift which changes the individual into the universal man and back again. But both men succeed in enlisting our own questioning selfhood, so that by virtue of the fact that they are standing in our stead, we readily see ourselves in their place. They speak to us but also on our behalf.

Here as always the question about destiny is concerned with the unfathomed mystery of the existing individual—a mystery that cannot be merely meaningless since it uncovers even in the question something of the answer which is expected. Kierkegaard previews, as it were, the conclusion of atheistic existentialists such as Heidegger and Sartre. Existence is pictured on its manward side as involuntary and unbidden, compelled and not chosen. What did I have to do with my own coming into the world? Is life itself, then, something into which I am merely "chucked" or thrown without so much as being asked? Yet at the same time I am given leave to exist, allowed to be. Who has done this? One would like to tell him a thing or two.

As a scientist Pascal is far more aware than Kierkegaard of the surrounding mystery of nature, for he is feeling the first shock of the Copernican revolution, as Kant was to call it a century later. Whether he speaks in his own person or not, his words in one celebrated sentence well define the natural finiteness of man: "These eternal spaces frighten me." Man, this odd mid-point between everything and nothing, who is he? Pascal's mathematical mind is struck by the sheer contingency, or might-have-been-otherness, of everyman. And being in addition a devout Christian, Pascal finds the question about destiny still more deeply underscored. It remains a mystery in which we are included, not a problem to be solved by one's own efforts.

By way of anticipation let me point out that for Pascal and

Kierkegaard the very asking of this question presupposes its answerability. In other words, the question about destiny is put to destiny itself, or rather to the "director" who alone can hear and reply to the question. It would seem, then, that a questionable destiny carries within itself the suggestion of an answerable, and answering, Providence. But before we follow up this suggestion, we must look a bit more closely at the question's nearer side, the way it reveals itself in human life.

III

It has a certain twofold character, the question about destiny, rather like a magnetic field set up by opposing yet interacting poles. The first pole is intensively emotional in nature, and its name is anxiety. This human attitude is well known to counselors and analysts and has received a large amount of clinical description in our day.[4] Anxiety has a recognizable structure which can be detected rather easily in people who are mentally ill and under treatment, but its symptoms are by no means confined to them. They are also apparent in the neurotic edginess and jittery agitation so widespread at the present time, especially in the Western world.

Perhaps the commonest danger signal for most of us is the sense of being under pressure, which may soon become unmanageable because of the multiplying of claims and linkages to which we are subjected almost incessantly. This may partly arise from the fact that the more we have to rely upon others to get things done, the greater is the risk of failure or nonfulfillment of our own desires. Again, the occasion of anxiety may be technological instead of social. As human life grows more and more mechanized, it tends of course to lose its sense of personal purpose and responsibility. However the feeling arises, the result is that we are harried, driven,

---

[4] See, for example, Rollo May, *The Meaning of Anxiety* (New York: The Ronald Press Co., 1950).

sharpened—whittled down, as it were, to innumerable contact points which tend to become friction points as well. Hence come stomach ulcers, nervous breakdowns, heart attacks, and usually in the time of life when people should be happily engaged in raising families or getting into good vocational stride. Hence, too, come book burning, witch-hunting, character assassination, not to mention still more sinister perils to our corporate health.

Plunged into a milieu like this, is it any wonder that our children should be "born tired"? Almost at once they are brought into the cross fire of an unrelenting barrage of stimuli, caught in a welter of confusing and even contradictory pressures which are bound to make each stage of life a veritable age of anxiety. Thus not only adolescence but also childhood and infancy suffer the blight of premature adulthood, while middle age becomes, in Aldous Huxley's caustic phrase, a period of "post-maturity."

It is valuable to remember that people long before us have known and had to face up to the nagging worries brought on by the lack of life's material necessities. Obviously, care about how one is going to be fed, clothed, housed, or given social status is the common lot of folk in every culture. When Jesus told his hearers, "Be not anxious," he was probably thinking of such proximate uncertainties as these. But anxiety as we feel it today means a great deal more than care or worry alone, however much these may be involved. In fact it bears a close resemblance to those inner demons which Jesus moved to exorcise by the miracle of faith, and which according to him could come out only by prayer and fasting.

Anxiety is sometimes confused with fear, but it ought not to be as it goes deeper down into the subsoil of our feelings. Fear, unlike anxiety, has concrete and nameable objects in view. It is a reaction provoked by definite threats and specific enemies—real or imaginary —against which an individual must and can take steps to guard himself. In the light of earlier discussion let us note that fear is an emotional problem whereas anxiety is an emotional mystery. The latter is not so much a threat as the very state of being threatened, the sense of being put upon by vague and hostile forces. Anxiety therefore borders upon the vacuous and the abysmal; it faces a nameless, faceless dread. One who is anxious is afraid not so much of others as of himself.

Worries about the cares and chores of daily life, and recurring fears about hostilities openly declared or nursed in secret, are but shadows thrown across man's path by this deep-rooted anxiety, tersely defined by Tillich as "finitude, experienced as my own finitude." [5] In order to communicate this lived reality, painters and poets in our day have had to employ nightmarish, surrealist symbols—bleeding limbs, gaping tombs, hooded faces, and the rest. Or they have used images like the "abyss," which produces dizziness or nausea in the one who must look down into it. It comes with something of a surprise to discover that the Bible employs similar tokens of anxiety—the desolate pit, the miry bog, the flying arrow, the deep waters, the shadowed valley, and many others. Both sets of images speak to the condition of contemporary men and women in the sharpest possible way.

The feeling of anxiety may take two forms. Either one is haunted by the sense of being hemmed in, or trapped, or boxed in by the abyss; or one may seem to be dangling in existence, condemned to live without cause and without means of support, visible or invisible. The first of these suggests confinement or enclosure, as in Sartre's play *No Exit;* the second portrays, rather, openness and a queasy rootlessness which lacks any anchorage in being. Both types are frequently reported in the clinical literature on this subject.

Each type, however, comes finally down to the same thing. A

[5] *The Courage to Be* (New Haven, Conn.: Yale University Press, 1952), p. 35.

question is taking shape and gathering a kind of terrible momentum: Who am I, really? Why am I at all? What am I to being? Does what I know not, also know me not? For when a man experiences finiteness as his own, he is in effect bringing the entire universe to trial. He is asking Being to justify itself; he may even, without intending to, be calling upon God.

Such stark anxiety is not assuaged, moreover, by fleeing into some new social collectivity; for what is this but a kind of pulverized self-destruction? We may, as Marcel has remarked, be heading into a society in which freedom would simply mean making oneself insignificant enough to escape the notice of the bosses; but this will not remove anxiety. For it would only throw back at us the same old question, Who am I? Whenever human mutuality turns into a hard, briquettelike uniformity, anxiety must be accentuated, not resolved.

Nor can a more refined sort of psychological probing lay this particular kind of ghost, since it could only add to our knowledge of the ignorance against which we are vainly struggling. Granted that a childhood trauma may often be removed by being exposed for what it is, but what may be done for one who is himself in a state of exposure? And it does not help to be told by social pathologists that others are in like case, that my predicament is general, unless together with these others I am able to establish real communion which transcends and absorbs anxiety.

It is important to notice how many people who have undergone extended psychiatric treatment should emerge from it with a certain hollow brittleness, as if having once been patched up, they do not propose to be hurt again. This is not true of all, to be sure; yet it happens often enough to give us pause. May it not be because they have been treated problematically, repaired instead of healed or made truly whole? In such cases the mystery of human destiny is still present; one has only been innoculated against it so that anxiety is not overcome but merely held at arm's length. Indeed, such people may be even more self-protective than before, and thus more deeply anxious.

No one wishes to be thought ungrateful to psychoanalysis, which has isolated and probed anxiety with such clinical exactness. But a considerable question remains whether it can ever be cured by these means. For anxiety cannot be "purely psychological"; it is also, and chiefly, "ontological" as Tillich and others keep saying. That is, it has to do with what is real, arises in the presence of the real, and is from first to last about the real. One wonders sometimes whether the psychiatrist may not simply drain off anxiety to a deeper level, which only postpones man's "rendezvous with destiny." This may not always or necessarily be so; but it seems to happen whenever it is forgotten that the question of my being-in-the-world is *ipso facto* one about Being, too. It asks about my station in the "Scheme of Things entire."

Another feature that is strongly marked in the state I am now describing has to do with guilt. At the heart of anxiety there often dwells the suspicion that one deserves just what he is getting from reality. Here, once again, it is useless to try to eradicate guilt feelings by explaining their connection with the violation of some cultural taboos, because their roots usually lie much further down. One thing is certainly clear about guilt: it is not explained by being explained away, and still less is it overcome.

Furthermore, a guilt-ridden person may be helped to disentangle himself from the complex which has been making him miserable without thereby becoming innocent again. In fact, there is no such thing as innocence *again*. Do not the Gospels warn against the dangers involved in mere house cleaning of the unclean spirits that tear and rend a man? Any such evacuation is simply an invitation to still more occupancy, so that the "last state of that man becomes worse than the first" (Matt. 12:43-45; see also Luke 11:24-26). Incidentally, this is why the early Christian apostles regarded evangelism as the necessary ally of exorcism, and why Jesus saw faith not as the result but as the requirement of miraculous cure.

The point to be made, however, is that anxiety very often involves accountability. One may not know for what or to whom he is held responsible, and yet the feeling persists. That is, he sees his destiny not as a chance upheaval or tiny disturbance in reality but as an affliction and possibly a curse. Once this line of thought is followed, it becomes difficult not to wonder whether this affliction may not also be an infliction, something which must be endured because it is sent. This, I take it, is the profound and shaking apprehension behind human guilt. Something in Being holds us answerable for our own failure to be—and particularly for the failure we cannot help, since in it our lapse from Being is most acutely and plainly revealed.

All this is by way of reiterating that anxiety has very much to do with Providence as well as destiny. It is haunted by the unclear image of the "director" who purposes and plans the course of human events. Hence the true antidote to anxiety is most emphatically not the suave assurance, "God will help you relax," so much in vogue with some popular preachers at this moment. Rather, it is to be found in the confidence that it is God who knows and cares and is powerful to save—a confidence that no event can shake and which even anxiety cannot in the end dislodge.

IV

The second pole of the question about destiny is the moral one, and its proper name is ambiguity. Usually this word has a logical reference, being employed to mean the equivocal character of a statement that can be taken in either of two different ways. To be sure, propositions are sometimes ambiguous, but still more so are the people who make them; this makes ambiguity a moral quite as much as a semantic matter.

Both the words and actions of men can be taken two ways; they are open to double interpretation. This occasions the foreboding that they may have their source in a duplicity within man himself. The churchman mentioned by Horace Walpole whose sanctity was equivocal can be matched by many others who reveal in their behavior a similar slippery two-sidedness. And who is not aware from time to time of this same odd duplicity in himself? Wanting to eat one's cake and have it too, making the worse appear the better reason—in every one of us there is this odd ambiguity which makes man what Pascal rightly called him, a chimera, an incomprehensible monstrosity.

No Christian thinker in our generation has been more assiduous than Reinhold Niebuhr in tracking down this moral ambiguity in man. Every sort of human behavior is touched by it, even the noblest and highest. Thus the will to live becomes the will to power—a transformation that is bound up within the very energizing of the will to stay alive. So self-preservation may turn quickly into aggression; I fight my enemy not merely to keep him off but also to make him recognize my superior strength. Or if I attempt to make love the law of my living, must I not forthwith cease to love but merely obey? Again, if I should try to scale the higher altitudes of spiritual integrity, may I not soon find myself in the amusingly equivocal position of the monk who is supposed to have boasted of his own order, "In humility we can beat the world"? Self-contradiction, ambiguity, hypocrisy—this is a good share of what human living means.

It would seem, then, that we are destined to remain our own worst enemies, until we are at last overtaken by the final enemy, death. The higher we rise, the harder we fall. This is a theme upon which many contemporary variations have been played, and we shall be listening to some of them in the later chapters of this book.

One may, like Simone de Beauvoir, construct a whole ethics of ambiguity upon the base of a neo-Stoic despair or resignation, without of course relying upon the ancient Stoic's trust in *providentia*. Or one may follow Albert Camus in counseling revolt, which is itself ambiguous since it says both Yes and No to what is termed the absurd. Absurdity, like ambiguity, is a word that stresses the sheer irrationality of every human action, aim, or attitude. But absurdity means more than this; it is not a synonym for what is silly or ridiculous from a rational point of view. In fact the ethics of absurdity has given up any pretense that choices may be made or conduct judged from such a standard. What is meant, rather, is that reason is itself absurd, and that moral judgment is totally out of keeping with the real situation in which we have to live—one, that is, of utter and inescapable ambiguity, whatever our profession or our practice.

According to this line of thought nothing in human existence can be moral, if this means rightness or virtue. There can be no guarantee of safe-conduct, no "nicely calculated less and more" of goodness. For each decision taken by man simply betrays his basic indecision, so that it becomes impossible for him to avoid some measure of double-dealing. This view, in short, denies all sincerity to so-called moral actions, claiming that man is caught in a deadlock where he cannot will any good thing. It is certainly a cynical view and when its implications are drawn out, a nihilistic one as well.

In such a grim and sobering light the question about destiny returns with new and unparalleled force. "What is man?" "A useless passion," answers Sartre. Here it is as if all the old Christian insights about the frailty and finitude of man were retained but perverted, as if one had to believe in hell without believing in God, as if the question about one's being could be answered only in terms of nothingness.

Yet is there not something more to be said about this tangled and deceitful situation in which man finds himself? From ambiguity through absurdity the line leads on to the suspicion of arbitrariness in human destiny, and one can hardly say that destiny is arbitrary without thereby accusing God. Likewise, from contingency through complicity the line takes us toward some belief, however resentful, in an original and outraged rightness deep in the nature of things. Hence springs the strikingly "inverse theology" of atheistic existentialism today. Those who most emphatically cast doubt on Providence, denying God if not actually defying him, are the very ones who succeed in bringing God back to life in a surprising way. For if, as Sartre says, we are "condemned to be free," to live in this twilight zone of *double-entendre,* someone must have sentenced us. So the thought of a righteous God comes in, quite unexpectedly, through the back door of the question about destiny.

Now this is something we have noticed before, and we shall have occasion to make the same sort of observation throughout the course of this book. It would be far too easy and too simple to say that the denial of God in our time involves an unintended affirmation of him, but we can certainly say that one does not get rid of God merely by denying his existence or his relevance to human affairs. On the contrary, one thereby betrays the fact that he still has to do with God and Providence. Do not men like Heidegger, Sartre, and Camus assure us just a bit too enthusiastically that they have given up all belief in the divine determination of human destiny? If God is dead, as Nietzsche proclaimed almost a century ago, why not bury him and get it over with?

What anxiety and ambiguity in human life reveal is simply that we have not done with God, nor he with us. To be sure, only a Christian believer, or at least a religious person, would put the matter thus; but on this interpretation depends the very possibility of real conversation between faith and unfaith. The question is whether man can become anxious, in the sense I have described, without disclosing a strange reflex or inversion of belief in Providence. It is likewise a question whether ambiguity can be accepted as the human situation without some understanding, however shrunken and contorted, of the fact that we are actually sinners—bereft of God, apparently forsaken by him, yet still accountable to him.

The only cure for both moral ambiguity and emotional anxiety is faith in God as the Christian doctrine of Providence expresses it. The nature of that faith is what constitutes the theme of this book. But in drawing this first chapter to a close several things may be pointed out, partly by way of anticipation, partly with respect to the rather rocky path already under our feet.

One thing is this. The anxious and ambiguous condition of everyman today is not a token solely of our wretchedness, but also testifies to man's authentic and God-given greatness. How may I know myself to be finite if I do not know something more than finitude by which I judge my present plight? Or how can I sense the frustrating ambiguity of my behavior without condemning it as woefully inadequate, and whence does such a standard arise? Even when I try to put the blame on destiny, I am really bearing witness against myself. Really this capacity of finding myself wanting is a most mysterious thing. For even in our cognizance of wretchedness and misery and exposure there is caught a glimpse of our true grandeur under God, a greatness not at all merited but bestowed, and thus the more remarkable.

Another point to be held in mind is this. Whatever reply a Christian believer in Providence finally gives to the question about destiny, it must be such as to meet and match the full force of the question. Surely Nicolas Berdyaev is correct in saying that many traditional doctrines of Providence actually "constitute the chief hindrance to belief in God" and even lead people into atheism, because their "dreadfully strained and artificial explanations" can only result in outright rebellion against any kind of religious faith.[6] When this occurs, it is because the framers of these doctrines have not really heard the question asked to which they pretend to have the answer. It is obvious that if Providence is indeed the Christian answer to the ambiguity and anxiety bound up in human destiny, then it must be shown and not merely said to be in very truth that answer.

And in the third place we not only must but can do this. Our faith in God's providence is by no means an evasion of the froward, bitter facts of life. Rather, as we shall see, it means entering into life's essential and irreducible mystery. And what is even more to the point, it is these same facts which make belief in Providence both necessary and possible. Necessary since by proving our own weakness they may serve to throw us back on God's strength; they dislodge us from vain, illusory self-confidence which drives ever deeper the wedge between us and God. And possible, too, because these facts humble and gentle us into accepting life as truly given, that is, initiated and intended by him who has it all within his keeping and who at the end will win our battles and his own. Our purpose in the succeeding chapters is to show the truth which inspired these lines of Dietrich Bonhoeffer:

Who am I? They mock me, these lonely questions of mine.
Whoever I am, Thou knowest, O God, I am Thine![7]

---

[6] *The Beginning and the End* (New York: Harper & Bros., 1952), pp. 151-53.
[7] *Prisoner for God: Letters and Papers from Prison* (New York: The Macmillan Co., 1953), p. 165. Used by permission of the publisher.

2

Concerning Fate

Thy way was in the sea,
And thy paths in the great waters,
And thy footsteps were not known.

—*Ps. 77:19 (A.S.V.)*

There is a way of putting the question about destiny as if it were no real question at all. It holds simply that destiny is identical with something called fate. Although fate is proposed as the answer, it is actually no more than an attenuated and aggravated form of the original question. Or rather, it is a way of not hearing the question, of precluding it, since it is based upon a complete refusal to accept the promissory note of any kind of faith. Is it not the very nature of fatalism to regard human destiny as a foregone conclusion, a book that is closed before it has even been opened?

Nevertheless, this supposed solution to the riddle of destiny must be looked into with extreme sympathy and care, if only because it seems so plausible to folk in our day. Karl Heim, several decades ago, observed that it was fate which expressed more than any other term the direction in which men were looking for the meaning of life. His statement still holds true. If we are going to reaffirm the providential understanding of our destiny, we shall have to meet as squarely and fully as we can the oppressive, enigmatic character of life which goes by the name of fate.

I

Let us say then without too much fear of being contradicted that fate is a powerful contemporary substitute for the providence of God. As a matter of fact, are not a great many professing Christians in reality but practicing fatalists? Their very eagerness to be reassured of Providence is itself a telling index of how remote and tenuous any such conviction is for them. In all candor does it not become increasingly difficult to find in either public policy or private motive more than the merest vestige of the faith that God guides, guards, and governs us? In any case there are surely multitudes of people, whether in or outside churches, who have a very fuzzy and and hazy working notion of Providence but betray an appallingly plain and practical notion of fate.

And what, really, does fate mean? Like most age-old words it has come to signify many different things. In every instance, however, fate names in an inclusive, comprehensive way those outer boundaries of our existence that seem to circumscribe and press upon man. It denotes that strange and spectral something which controls, determines, hedges, about the life of man, overriding our wishes and disregarding our needs. As in the tragic plays of Aeschylus, Euripides, and Sophocles, fate broods unrelentingly and tauntingly over everything human. In terms of fate each human situation is a "border-situation," which makes it an encounter with nothingness, in Helmut Kuhn's phrase. Life fronts upon the alien and the forbidding according to this fatalistic interpretation.

This view of life moves somewhat uncertainly between identifying fate with doom and equating it with sheer chance or fortune. The first hints darkly at inevitability and necessity; the second stresses what is accidental, unpredictable, and hence inscrutable. But the first is plainly fundamental to the second. On the fatalistic hypothesis man's vulnerability to chance is finally seen as the effect of doom upon him, so that what is accidental is thought in the last analysis to be ultimately and insurmountably necessary to man. The word "fate" itself means that which is decreed or spoken, which cannot be taken back but must be carried out or executed. Thus fate is put forward as an explanation of human situations such as ambiguity or anxiety, and becomes what we may call the principle of the finality of finitude. Need it be repeated that this is the kind of "answer" which permits no question to be raised? That is, it voices the belief that the issues of life are decided in advance, decided moreover against our self-fulfillment.

Again, fatalism attributes to all border situations an emphatically unitary and even arbitrary character; in them it makes bold to see the outlines of a single, monolithic, all-determining shape. Still more, it asserts that an almighty No is spoken against every longing or endeavor that can be called man's own—spoken in permanent and irrevocable contradiction to every human Yes. Because of this I think we might call fate a sort of Providence-in-reverse, which is to say a malevolent, teasing parody of God's guiding, guarding, governing power.

Do you think this is all very far from life today? Then mark these words written by a young American about himself and his contemporaries: "'This is really a *beat* generation,'" he says. "Most than mere weariness, it implies the feeling of having been used, of being raw. It involves a sort of nakedness of mind, and, ultimately, of soul. . . . In short, it means being undramatically pushed up against the wall of oneself." [1] That has been the actual experience of more folk than one likes to think of, and it is a potent breeding ground of our contemporary fatalism.

This sense of being passive pawns caught in the "fell clutch of circumstance" encourages a definition of fate as being, quite exactly,

[1] Clellon Holmes, "This Is the Beat Generation," *New York Times Magazine,* November 16, 1952, p. 10.

that which we human beings can do nothing about. The fatalities of life happen to us even though they may take place within us—so that pain and sorrow and frustration are regarded as the burden imposed upon man. It is instructive to observe that although fatalism usually begins by distinguishing between what man can control and what he cannot, it ends up by absorbing the former into the latter—which obviously makes nonsense out of the initial distinction.

Yet human life does not simply come to a standstill when it encounters fate. It may become only more energetic and defiant, like the buzzing fly trapped in my closed hand or like the young hot-rod driver mentioned by Clellon Holmes, "eating up the highway at ninety miles an hour, and steering with his feet." The French existentialist writers have been telling us that the proper name for this behavior in the presence of fate is revolt. Now revolt is both a No and a Yes; it can perhaps be best described as a resigned refusal. In a significant study, Albert Camus has shown that revolt is a complex response to fate; based upon a keen awareness of my own positive worth as a man, it nonetheless is the flinging of myself into the teeth of fate—not as a sacrifice but rather as a sort of hostage to it.[2] If it is not too complicated to say so, revolt both affirms and denies fate; it affirms what it denies and denies what it affirms, namely the self who revolts, resignedly, against fate.

From this twisted, tortured thinking there arises the intriguing idea that only revolt is pure—a theme on which Simone de Beauvoir has been writing. Pure, that is, because it is unhampered by prudential calculations and devious self-righteousness; pure, again, because it has about it an ecstatic and almost dedicated quality that spurns all compromise and convention. According to the fatalist we never live half so intensely or integrally as when we are fighting what is

[2] See *The Rebel* (New York: Alfred A. Knopf, Inc., 1954), especially the first chapter.

bound to beat us in the end. (At this moment I am waiting with my fellow New Englanders for the probable onslaught of a heavy hurricane; I must confess that the preceding sentence makes considerable sense to me, who am not a fatalist.) There is a remarkable example of this in the character named Santiago in Hemingway's *The Old Man and the Sea,* who catches the biggest fish of his life and after almost superhuman struggling with the sharks manages to bring to shore only the bones they have picked clean. The meaning of this parable should not be too difficult; it is by straining ourselves to the limit we come to know the nature of that limit; success and failure are finally the same. There is no more telling witness to the tragic hold of fate upon us, says the fatalist, than our own vain and frenzied efforts to escape its all-encompassing control.

II

Puppets may dangle on the strings of fate, but human beings are not puppets. They are rather Pinocchios, puppets who come alive, ask saucy questions, make their own mistakes, try to set the world to rights. They also make at times a mighty effort to weave some web of meaning out of the same events in which they are themselves enmeshed. So it happens that men do more than react to what is fateful in existence; they must perforce also reflect upon it.

When this reflection is carried on outside the Christian faith, the fatalities of life are customarily thought of as all-including and all-compelling. Thus men come to believe, even though they might prefer not to, that there is a strange power which sets bounds to our struggling even as it provokes and aggravates our struggling, bringing it down to nothing in the end. Whatever the right name of such a power may be, it is obviously not God.

In recent years a myth has been going the rounds in western Europe that expressees both man's immediate refusal and his ultimate resignation in the face of what he takes to be his fate. It is the old story of Sisyphus, a king of Corinth who was punished for his greed on earth by having to perform a frustrating sort of penance in Hades. He had to roll uphill a great stone which always came hurtling down just as he approached the summit and so had to be rolled up again. To writers such as Camus, Sisyphus has become the "hero of absurdity," symbolizing man himself, who is condemned to do endlessly futile things in an endlessly futile world. But modern Sisyphus, unlike his ancient prototype, does not have even the meager solace that eternal justice is being done to sanction his suffering. No, this is just the way things always have been, are, and always will be, world without end—and it goes without saying that there is no amen.

There are some people on the American side of the Atlantic who still insist that these symbols and slogans of revolt abroad are at worst a literary posturing for effect or at best a quite understandable overintoxication with crisis and catastrophe. But do they not have deeper reasons? Our present-day preoccupation with fate is the consequence of the general evacuation of God from the scene of human affairs. Not many years ago Jean-Paul Sartre's play *The Devil and the Good Lord* opened in Paris. It showed itself to be astute theater with considerable dramatic drive. It also proved to be a very forthright and rather bitter working out of the author's own categorical denial of God. The main motif was put into the mouth of Goetz, an ambiguous fellow described as the "buffoon of evil" and the "imposter of good." At one point in the play he says, "There's no argument; I tell you, God is dead. . . . I have this war to fight and I shall fight it." Later in a review Paul Ricoeur commented that while the play added nothing new to Sartre's well-known philosophy, it did provide a "sort of frightening exhibition of the silence and the absence of God."

Returning after hearing and reading such things to the comfortable clutter and clatter of life at home, the American traveler is tempted at once to put such distressing thoughts quite out of his head. The old hum of smoothly functioning well-being all around is still to be heard. Really God cannot be too far away. People are generally smiling, hurrying, busy—

> Engaged in devising the perfect refrigerator,
> Engaged in working out a rational morality,
> Engaged in printing as many books as possible,
> Plotting of happiness and flinging empty bottles.[3]

It surely cannot be as bad as we had supposed over there, we say.

After a few days, however, one has a horrid second thought. The situation may be every bit as bad—and possibly even worse—just because we do not realize how bad it is. Looking more intently at our mode of life, does not one discover something very like the stoical resolve of Goetz, the tragic "you can't win" of the fisherman Santiago, or the aching self-defeat of Sisyphus? Here too, it seems, the fateful powers are at work; may not the very magnitude of our collective operations constitute a kind of revolt against these powers? We may not be so shrill as our European contemporaries in declaring that God is absent and silent, but one could hardly say that by and large we are witnessing in the comings and goings of daily life to God's living word and providential presence.

Once in a penetrating discussion of Faulkner's novel *The Sound and the Fury,* Sartre himself noted that its characters simply "did what they were going to do as if it had already been done." *That* is the gist of fatalism, whether lived or thought. And it is not at all necessary that we turn to drama and fiction for evidence of the current fatalistic trend. Anyone who counsels folk in personal difficulty knows how deep this strain runs and how readily it may come to the surface. Gabriel Marcel puts his finger on the matter

---

[3] From "The Rock," by T. S. Eliot. Used by permission of Harcourt, Brace and Company, Inc.

when he says that "life is being less and less felt as a gift to be handed on, and more and more felt as a kind of incomprehensible calamity, like a flood, against which we ought to be able to build dikes." [4] In one area after another we seem to get caught in the traps of our own devising, victimized by the very tools by which we shaped our mastery, brought low precisely by what seemed to exalt us. Yes, we have contributed in our peculiarly American manner to the well-nigh total eclipse of God. The shadow of fate grows darker and deeper by the day and hour. If we lack genuine faith in the living, speaking, working God, our destiny becomes our doom.

III

Fatalism is of course a very old as well as very new viewpoint toward human destiny. But those who lived in pre-Christian Greece and Rome had fate and heaven too—they kept their gods while putting fate above them. Since the gods themselves were believed to exist within the range and reckoning of fate, they possessed a fellow feeling and compassionate knowledge of mortal life. Fate might have the last word but not the only word about man's destiny. Its force was channeled, mediated, as it were refracted through the agency of divinities too numerous to mention, beings who kept on the whole a fairly benign watchfulness with regard to man. Between men and the gods there seems to have operated a quite comfortable *quid pro quo* sort of arrangement, celebrated in rite and story, by which shining devotion to human causes and a somber doubt touching the ultimate reality were able to dwell and work together in man's spirit.

Ancient popular religion could even go so far as to personify fate—Clotho, who spins the skein of life; Lachesis, who measures

[4] *Man Against Mass Society* (Chicago: Henry Regnery Co., 1952), p. 70.

it out; and Atropos, who cuts it. On such terms as these one might discover something almost human in the reign of fate; one might actually become enamored of its fascinating reality, as the recurring theme of *amor fati* in Latin literature shows—a theme, by the way, which lingers on in Nietzsche many centuries later. Most of all in the great tragic poets of the Periclean Age this whole conception of fate was absorbed and largely neutralized within the growing belief that Zeus, the god of justice, ruled supreme in heaven and over the earth.

The entire context in which sophisticated writers believe in fate today, however, is a very different one indeed. This view of human existence calls itself frankly "post-Christian"; it urges that we put fate in the place of the nonexistent—and also nonessential —God. Fate is offered to us as the only possible substitute for God— possible, that is, to anyone who knows what the world is about —and is recommended to fill the vacuum which God has left behind him. It is the right word for what up to now benighted men and women have mistakenly been calling God.

Here is no personification at all, no *amor fati,* no confidence in compassionate, kindred powers between ourselves and fate. There is only what Hölderlin called "earth's heavy burden of fatality." The bleak outlook that repudiates Christian faith in exchange for fatalism sees the human being alone in an alien universe, surrounded on every hand by barriers which appear to be closing in upon him; this encroachment is interpreted, as it is experienced, as a kind of final up-againstness. So-called post-Christian fatalism is not even connected with its classical prototype by lineal descent, for it is rather a reconstructed and reactivated fatalism serving a very different purpose in an equally different culture. We might in fact call it an archaic, abstract neopaganism. This is why its pronouncements have a nightmarish and abysmal character which accurately mirrors the surrealist type of experiences out of which they emerge.

This is a position taken by those people in our time who have made a basic decision to regard existence and destiny as inexorable.

How then shall we deal with the issues that are posed for us by such a view of life? That is, how may we give a more adequate and valid interpretation of what is fateful in life while remaining loyal to the God whose will and way we know in Jesus Christ? First, let us freely grant that nothing in our Christian faith excuses us from having to face and think through that which causes others to accept fatalism. A Christian's life is just as precarious and vulnerable to destructive power as any other sort of life. We live as much at the beck of disaster and are equally prey to the claims of despair. There is, to be sure, a genuine security and serenity which faith in God brings; but it ought not to be confused with a magic island of refuge, a privileged immunity, or a pair of seven-league boots for overstepping the boundaries with which all human life is hedged. Who knows the fragile nature of mortality better than the Christian believer? Can the fatalist possibly know it half so well? What makes this sense so poignant and impassioned in Christianity, however, is just that it is evoked by a still deeper and contrasting sense—that fatality is not the final word about our life, nor even about our death. It is only in the light of God, and of faith in him, that human life can be judged vain or futile; and in that light we do not overlook but rather go forth to meet the unwelcome, unbidden facts about our earthly destiny.

Secondly, although we Christians do not *believe* in fate, we can quite easily understand why others might do so. Unlike classical polytheism our faith does not consider fate to be above God. Over against neo-pagan fatalism Christianity declares that fate is only a spurious ersatz of God, which usurps a place it cannot really fill. Our belief is rather that life's border situations stand under God, therefore between man and God. For this reason the word "fate" is not in our proper Christian vocabulary at all. But we know what is meant by those who use the word, because we stand with them in the communion of bewilderment and suffering.

Again, the Christian sees the fateful boundaries of human life as truly compelling man but never as coercing God. They constitute real barriers against undue self-confidence on our part; they keep us in our proper place before God; they even help us to rely on him more and more completely. Thus we cannot believe that what is fateful is as compulsive for God as it is for us. How can it be so if it is actually the means by which God enlists and strengthens our faith in him? And so the persuasion grows that our very barriers are God's frontiers through which he comes righteously and graciously to bring his saving power to our aid. We, of course, cannot see the fatalities of our existence as they must appear to God; and yet it is our Christian duty to meet and understand these things by faith in him to whom they are neither final nor irrevocable.

Something like this must be in our minds as we prepare to answer contemporary fatalism. We are bound to declare that fate is no real substitute for an absent, silent God, but rather a blasphemous parody of him. Let us be very clear that fatalism is at bottom nihilism; it comes down to that. Yet for this reason it raises in a most acute and unavoidable way the whole question about Providence. That is why it cannot be shrugged off as "atheism" and henceforth dismissed. True, the proponents of this point of view press its claims boldly, at times with an exaggerated theatricality, but always too with an unbearable lucidity. Moreover, they are not content simply to describe the vacuum where God used to be; as has been said, having abandoned God, they are now trying to imitate him by creating a world out of nothing. But only God can thus create the world. Actually the fatalist is not so much a denier as a defier of God. He is, in short, a blasphemer; and blasphemy has meaning only if God himself is somewhere within hearing distance.

The message of Providence can scarcely come into this situation genially and blandly. It is not to be administered like a pat on the back or whistled like a cheery tune in the dark. Only as we have learned to take the full, exhausting measure of the worst, have we the right to say the providential best about our human destiny. But we must not on this account hesitate or temporize, for this great message is both opportune and pertinent. More than fourteen hundred years ago from a prison cell in Pavia, Boethius set forth with eloquent clarity the true relation between Providence and what men call fate. He wrote:

The Divine mind, . . . placed in the castle of its own simplicity, hath determined manifold ways for doing things; which ways being considered in the purity of God's understanding, are named Providence, but being referred to those things which He moveth and disposeth, they are by the ancients called Fate. . . . So that all that is under Fate is also subject to Providence, to which also Fate itself obeyeth. . . . That which departeth farthest from the first mind is involved more deeply in the meshes of Fate, and everything is so much the freer from Fate, by how much it draweth nigh to the hinge of all things.[5]

What may be called the providential principle is plainly focused in this passage. Belief in Providence, far from being a mere rubbing out of what is truly fateful about human destiny, is in truth its radical re-evaluation in the light of faith. This does not mean its dismissal altogether from the realm of thought, any more than its disappearance from the scene of life. But it means that fate has not for God the same reality it has to us, and that therefore we can take it in our human stride in the confidence that fate stands

[5] *The Consolation of Philosophy*, Bk. IV.

45

under God, as we mortals stand under fate. In fact, the entire doctrine of Providence is somehow gathered up within these words, "under God."

IV

Let us now drive deeper into the heart of the issue between fatalism and the Christian view of Providence. Perhaps what has already been said can be summed up in this way: we must accept fatality, or the fateful, as the limited, encroaching condition of our existence, but not fatalism as the true understanding of our destiny. Exactly what this means will grow clearer if we allow our thinking to be guided by two verses from the apostle Paul which form indeed the biblical basis of this great doctrine: "For I am sure that neither death, nor life, nor angels, nor principalities, nor things present, nor things to come, nor powers, nor height, nor depth, nor anything else in all creation, will be able to separate us from the love of God in Christ Jesus our Lord" (Rom. 8:38-39). Logically this may seem a negative sort of statement indeed, but theologically it is a most positive one. In each instance a real threat or peril to ourselves is recognized, yet its final power to separate us from God is repudiated. Here is a truly affirmative denial—a summons to face reality which at the same time refuses to surrender, or go down before it.

Paul's catalogue of things that indeed may but cannot finally separate us from God begins with death, man's last enemy, lying in wait around this corner or the next to level and destroy. Even harder to bear than death is the fear of death which shadows us all through life. Poetry, writes Richard Eberhart, is a "spell against death"; so too, he might have pointed out, are marriage and the family, commerce, statecraft, education, and religion itself. And what is worse, the fear of death is compounded with the abysmal anxiety of guilt—as if we believed we had death coming to us. "The wages of sin is death"; in some sense too persistent to be dismissed, death is the "pay-off," the price of wrongness in our life. Thus Athanasius long ago observed that death is so inherently bound up with sin that what is sinful can become sinless only through a process of dying. More than simply a part of the Christian gospel, such a truth is part of the subterranean anguish deeply felt in man's own consciousness of himself. Yet it is the Christian faith which catches up and savingly transforms this generally felt connection between sin, death, and guilt. Since death must always mean for us the cross of Christ, it can be borne, accepted, even gloried in, as belonging within the mysterious economy of God. Faith does not overleap or circumvent death but sees right through it and beyond it to an austerely loving Providence.

Then there is life itself, writes Paul, by which he surely means the dynamic, vital force that moves us forward, sometimes keeping even the terrible thought of death at bay. Paul knows very well that life may easily become separated from its Alpha and Omega, more especially when it seems to be running along nicely under its own power. Then our very prayers for strength or courage take on the guise of stimulants or tonics, self-concerned and self-administered. Does not the whole machinery of religion sometimes get devoted to the end of making God unnecessary for sustaining life, as God is thought to be merely instrumental to our vital needs and hopes? Religion is constantly being tempted to use God for man's own purposes, to domesticate him, bargaining with him for his power, and so wishing to rob God of his lordship over life. But a Christian does not need to be told that this is a perversion of true prayer and genuine faith. He understands that life means ultimately a gift, a trust, a charge to keep from God.

Many Protestants do not speak much of angels any more, though they still bother us a bit at Christmas and Easter. But in these latter days we know perhaps a good deal more than Paul did about principalities and powers, for the feeling runs very strong among us that we are being carried along and swallowed up in vast historic tides to which as human beings we make not the slightest difference. We come to believe that we count only as votes, numbers, tools. Our very names tend more and more to be tags and labels, convenient handles for collective manipulation. The upshot is that identity itself becomes nonentity.

Right here lies the greatest obstacle to belief in Providence for many in our day, and it must be faced. This crushing sense of human insignificance is not of course a new thing, but today it has a quite unheard-of range and force. The folk of this generation around the world have seen the systematic collectivizing and vicious brutalizing of men on a scale far greater than ever before; they have not only endured but participated in ghastly horrors and demonic actions without number. Scars like these do not heal easily or quickly. A friend recalls a terrible day back in Estonia when Russian soldiers were herding political prisoners into two freight trains standing on adjacent tracks but headed in opposite directions, waiting to take these people to Siberia or the Ukraine. What, you may ask, could Providence have meant to such wretched victims or to their helpless fellow countrymen who watched nearby?

Yet the strange thing was that Providence did mean something, for they were shouting the words of the twenty-third psalm as the trains pulled out. Those who prayed the Lord's Prayer in Dachau and Buchenwald bore a similar witness, as did individuals such as Hanns Lilje, Bishop Berggrav, Dietrich Bonhoeffer and Martin Niemöller. Perhaps, indeed, it takes imprisonment or worse to make Providence meaningful—the conviction that God cares for everyone as if he cared for each alone. In any case the visitation of such principalities and powers does not drive men further from God necessarily but may serve mysteriously to draw men even closer to God.

With Paul the apostle, we might go on to speak of time, the

"riddle of the road," to which a later chapter will be given, or of those sudden shifts from exaltation to despondency that seem to be our lot. We could even add our own particular frustrations to the list—those lurking, prowling enemies of our integrity and peace. Yet surely the providential principle is beginning to emerge already. It is that the same things which hide God possess also the mysterious faculty of disclosing him, so that we are able to discover Providence in just those situations from which all hope or help seems ruthlessly excluded. Our encounters with the fateful do not tell a single, fatalistic story. They are really and irreducibly mysterious.

Yes, what men have called fate is a mystery—it stands between ourselves and God. These things of which Paul speaks do mask God, as well as cloud our vision and imperil our effort. While therefore they must not be ignored or bypassed, neither can they be explained on their own terms. If they do not speak directly of God, it is also true that they do not speak merely for themselves. Just because the fateful occupies this middle distance between God and man, because it actually menaces our bond of communion with God, it cannot be taken as in any way equivalent to God.

But neither may we come in faith to God except through the dark valley and in the presence of our enemies, nor should we wish to do so. Must not the just man suffer much? Can the disciple be above his Lord, who was bruised for our iniquities and wounded for our transgressions? The element of sheer mystery within fatality may rebuff our knowledge, but it also elicits and confirms our faith. Since it is intermediate, may it not also be somehow instrumental to God's design and will? By what is fateful, therefore, "we are afflicted in every way, but not crushed; perplexed, but not driven to despair; persecuted, but not forsaken; struck down, but not destroyed" (II Cor. 4:8-9). Here again Paul states the providential principle with utmost precision: the power of saying this "but" to affliction, perplexity, persecution, defeat, resides alone in those who

49

are faithful to God; yet this power is called into play through the very situations it must overcome. Our courageous use of dark things is made possible by those things themselves, under God. Without the really fateful, Providence could never become for us a live option at all. And what is more, our "but" does not proceed simply from a fortitude which is part of our natural human selves; it is instead, this "but," drawn forth by something speaking to us from the other side of fate, or rather, by someone who uses fate as the occasion for making contact and establishing a closer fellowship with us.

Once more hear Blaise Pascal. "All things cover up some mystery," he wrote. "All things are the veils that cover God. Christians ought to recognize Him in all." His words are not stale platitudes; they were written to his elder sister after the death of their beloved father. Is not Pascal saying that our recognition of God is made possible through God's very disguises? Since in all things God may be hidden, may he not reveal himself in all? We can speak of a disguise or covering-up only if we are aware of what is thus disguised—yes, of a revealing that is vouchsafed through the disguise itself.

Furthermore, our recognition of God in the midst of apparent fate is really a mutual recognition in which God takes cognizance of us and refuses to allow us to become totally estranged from him. There at the barricades of destiny God notices and responds to us, challenging and correcting our little faith in him. So true is this that even our distrust of God is seen to be the result of a reluctance to accept life at his hands and on his terms. If we complain of God, we must, however, do our complaining *to* him; and our complaint is really a confession that we do not trust him to be God or make faithful response to him just where he is trying to break through to us. On this point Kierkegaard has written with customary discernment:

Complain! The Lord is not afraid, He is well able to defend Himself, but how might He be able to speak in His defense if no one ventures to complain as it is seemly for a man to do? Speak, lift up thy voice, speak aloud, God surely can speak louder, He possesses the thunder— but that too is an answer, an explanation, reliable, trustworthy, genuine, an answer from God Himself, an answer which even if it crush a man is more glorious than gossip and rumor about the righteousness of providence which are invented by human wisdom and circulated by effeminate creatures and eunuchs.[6]

This truth, that God encourages us to complain to him because he is fully able to justify himself, is a part of the Christian teaching about Providence which must not be overlooked. The Bible very frequently gives evidence of it, especially in the Psalms, but in the prophetic books and the Gospels as well. Characteristically, the man of the Bible is one who brings his troubles and resentments without hesitation before the Lord. He is as far as possible removed from the conventional picture of the pious person who would never think of questioning God.

There is a separation from God occasioned by our experience of what is fateful; but it is self-separation, the work of man and not of God. To question God, however, or to make complaint to him is not to deepen this gulf but rather to throw a bridge across it. Since every complaint against fate is in effect a complaint against God's way of governing his world, it is a *rapprochement* on our part toward him. And what we come to see by means of this approach is that our very doubt displays a surprising degree of implicit faith. There is a sense, indeed, in which only the man of faith can doubt bravely or complain strongly, "as it is seemly for a man to do." And the truth that God uses what is fateful for encouraging our doubt, as well as our faith, means that he takes cognizance of us in our

[6] *Op. cit.,* pp. 112-13. Used by permission of Princeton University Press.

estrangement from him, so that nothing in all creation, no matter how terrifying or tragic, is able to cut us off from his determining, and determined, love.

V

There is a maxim which puts quite precisely and positively what it means to believe in Providence within the context of apparent fate. Man's extremity, we sometimes say, is God's opportunity. I believe we can take these words quite seriously, making them with utter honesty our own; and I should like to show this by referring to certain human experiences of real extremity which in themselves are also instances of divine opportuneness.

For one thing, there is the experience of *being spared*. An earthquake in Lisbon, an airliner crashing against a mountain, or the fall of the bridge of San Luis Rey are events that ought to raise troubling questions about the providence of God. And in fact they do. But notice that such questioning becomes relevant for those who are left behind, who are not singled out for this apparently capricious treatment. And notice too that as the question grows, it takes a double form: not only, Why did the other have to die? but also, Why was I or someone else spared? Really, fatalism refuses either form of the question; it will not entertain the possibility of any "Why?" at all. It attempts to throw the question back at the questioner by declaring that such cruel happenings simply cannot be understood with reference to anything like reason or purpose; they must be not so much accepted as endured. And yet this double question is not easily silenced, even within fatalism itself, which is why fate seems to take on many of the attributes of God.

Far more is at stake here than the angry otherness of God, moreover. The question wrenched from us by sudden, inexplicable death means at least this—that God cannot be accused of one man's destruction unless he is also responsible for the safety of another.

If there were no fortuitousness in the world, no death by accident, there would of course be no need for Providence either. At any rate the thought of Providence would simply not have occurred to anyone who had not been threatened by its very contradiction. Actually, the anguished "Why?" that is often forced out by such events is more a prayer than a retort. It is an invitation to God to talk back and explain himself. As Seneca said to Lucullus, "You do not deny the existence of Providence, but only bring complaints against it." That, I believe, is profoundly true of all our protestations against fate. What we question about fate is not so much its inhuman and relentless character as its apparent capriciousness or arbitrariness. And this is already to go well beyond the hypothesis of fatalism toward something which begins more and more to look like Providence. Being spared must be accounted for, just as much as being chosen as the grim hostage of death. The two questions are bound up in one and the same event. And if we are spared, then we are saved, delivered from a similar destruction—how, by whom, and for what secret purpose?

In saying this, we have not answered the problem of fateful death; that is obvious. But have we not put ourselves in a place where its essential mystery can begin to speak to us? Where others write "fate," we do not simply substitute the "will of God"; for we do not claim to know enough for that. Rather, we affirm that what is humanly extreme may be divinely opportune, insofar as it drives us to put our questions to God and enables him to make mysterious reply. Another's death may serve me providentially by raising the issue of my own life's meaning under God, by leading me out of numbness and shock into deepened conversation with him. And this is very far from any kind of self-congratulation on a "near miss"; it sees that each of us exists only by the grace of God.

Again, consider the experience of *being sustained*. This comes to the fore most clearly, perhaps, in bereavement; but we also meet it in less tragic form. I have in mind chiefly the way in which a man or woman discovers unexpected reserves of strength, or as we say, catches a second breath, at the very point where strength is most depleted. There is in human beings a demonstrated capacity to take whatever comes and not to go to pieces under it which neither animal self-preservation nor disciplined toughness can adequately explain. True, in every human response to danger there must be something of the animal at bay, just as there must be something stoical in doggedly holding on to meaning in the face of mystery. But just as truly there is something more. In moments like these, when one is thrown sharply back upon his own resources, he often comes to realize that they are not his resources at all but are bestowed or made available to him from beyond himself. And then he does a great deal more than fight back; he clings in faith to what is threatening him. So Jacob cries, "I will not let thee go, except thou bless me"; Job affirms, "Though he slay me, yet will I trust in him"; and Jesus prays, "Nevertheless not my will, but thine, be done."

To be sure, one has to be out at the edge, alone, to feel most keenly this sense of being stayed or supported, allowed to go on living long after the very will to live may have vanished in despair. But is it in spite of fate or perhaps because of it that we are gifted with this resiliency of soul? Here once more our very peril takes a truly providential form. All that can knowingly be said is that in the presence of our enemies a table of nourishing grace is somehow laid, and that there is nearness to God even within the consciousness of distance from God.

Still another fairly normal experience is that of *being led*. It presupposes, obviously, not safety but danger. One cannot be aware of being led if he has never been threatened by lostness. Only to those aware of having lingered in what Dante calls the dark wood of life can this assuring experience manage to come.

It would in fact be altogether pointless and impossible without prior confusion, groping, and ignorance. It begins with the recognition, however dim, that one lacks the guidance he needs in order to resolve these difficulties. Yet this experience is not in any sense the successful resolution of them on one's own terms. It is rather that of being dependent upon illumination from another source, a source at once transcendent to and yet at the same time strangely ingredient within one's own thought and action.

It may be asked, "May one not simply be mistaken about this?" Perhaps what we call being led is no more than a complicated mode of conditioned reflex or a type of physical determination. Why be in a hurry to attribute to God what glands are perfectly able to do? It is of course impossible for Christian faith to give an answer which can satisfy the naturalist or the determinist, and yet we are not reduced to utter silence by this sort of question either. If we take our stand on the definition of human destiny as "centered selfhood" or "myself as given," then we must insist that man is self-directed at least to some extent. Our destiny is shaped not only by processes but by purposes as well. Herbert Butterfield, the British historian, writes of the history making that goes on above our heads, so to speak; and persons, even more than civilizations, feel the force of such a "manifest destiny." Without denying the determination of human life by subhuman powers, we know as men that this is not the whole story. There is always something more, and better, to be said. We are the sort of beings who are lured as well as pushed, led as well as driven.

Now this experience can honestly be regarded as a real taste of Providence. Plainly, it has nothing to do with the shallow optimism that once we trust in God, everything is bound to turn out happily for us. It is of course this pious superficiality which has rightly alienated many of our tough-minded contemporaries from the very idea of divine Providence, which they mistakenly associate with it.

We shall never be able to justify God's ways with man merely by
contradicting other views. It is only by admitting their measure of
truth and by allowing our premature generalizations to be corrected
by whatever evidence they put forward that we can know what
being led really means. It means, in short, that we are working
better than we know, because our life is in the keeping of that
which can do for us what we cannot do for ourselves.

It is naturally true that "being led" is a judgment passed upon
experience that is past rather than present. We are far more likely
to see God's hand at work in events long after they have happened
than while we are living through them. Thus a great deal in our
belief in Providence is retrospective, as when a person regards a
bitter mischance as beneficial in the long run. But he really does
see what really happened then, as its web of meaning is spun out in
time. So a woman whose wish to have a home of her own is denied
may come to look back upon that denial as indeed providential,
since it enabled her to find another, unsuspected kind of satisfaction.
Are we not right then to agree with Tillich that there is a "quality
of inner directedness present in every situation"? Yes, we may be
heartened by the conviction, solemn and serene, that

> Though Satan's wrath beset our path,
> And worldly scorn assail us,
> While Thou art near we will not fear;
> Thy strength shall never fail us.
> Thy rod and staff shall keep us safe,
> And guide our steps forever;
> Nor shades of death, nor hell beneath,
> Our souls from Thee shall sever.

Indeed, how otherwise than in man's extremity could God ever
seize the opportunity of reaching him in judgment and in mercy?
This is a lesson which life never ceases to teach us.

The kinds of human experience of which I have been speaking are all genuine border situations and confront what is actually fateful in our destiny. Yet each is also providential in the highest degree. Deliverance, buoyancy, guidance—these are not events for which we have to thank our lucky stars, but signs that the hard mold of so-called fate is cracking, that authentic light is sifting through the veil of mystery thrown up in front of God. They can only mean that a mighty Yes is spoken to us in the very midst of the nearer, louder No which seems to come from fate. And what is more, these sign-events do not represent simply the Christian believer's opinion as to what might just as easily be explained on other, utterly nonprovidential grounds. For they actually disclose and release a power to be which can only come from God. Thus human extremity gives God his opportunity, and by means of faith that opportunity becomes ours as well.

What began as a negation therefore issues in a powerful affirmation. Even though God's ways were not known, his path was in the great waters. For it is Providence that says Yes to us through the implacable No of would-be fate; and this is not our Yes but God's, who guides and guards and governs everything—yes, everything—for good.

3

Freedom—God's and Man's

"A man's heart deviseth his way: but the Lord directeth his steps."

—Prov. 16:9

Tucked away in the book of Proverbs, this brief verse catches up, as well perhaps as any in the Bible, what it means to believe in Providence. The words themselves are pious, unpretentious, almost trite. No great leader said them, and no historic occasion called them forth. This is only a popular adage, thrown off like a quiet spark from the anvil of common sense. And furthermore, the idea it embodies is by no means uniquely Christian, nor even distinctively biblical, but has been echoed many times in the folk wisdom of the world.

Yet what is really startling in these words is precisely their matter-of-factness; it is just their casual and representative, indeed anonymous, quality which compels our attention. Living as we do in a time when theologians have been laboring mightily to define and to defend an exclusively Christian sort of truth, it does us good to be reminded that our faith holds some convictions in common with the rank and file of mankind.

"A man's heart deviseth his way"—that means his freedom to make plans and act them out, to live his own life. "But the Lord directeth his steps"—that points us toward another sort of freedom, namely, God's right to be God, to have his way with us in all our downsittings and uprisings, our comings and goings. And Providence, whatever else it may mean, also means the structuring of a rapport between these two freedoms, God's and man's. It expresses the faith that God has what might be called a controlling interest in the course of our living from day to day, an interest on which we can rely and with which we may in some real measure co-operate.

Theology needs to find cleaner, truer ways of setting forth this relationship between divine and human freedom, which is Providence. Most of all, each of us ought to ask whether it is reasonable to believe in such a relationship at all. My purpose in this chapter is to give a not uncritical yet genuinely affirmative answer to this question.

I

The last chapter endeavored to stabilize the Christian doctrine of Providence against the fatalistic rendering of human destiny. There it was maintained that our experiences of the fateful are mysteriously open to another kind of interpretation and may even wear a decidedly providential aspect. So far, so good. But there is another way of conceiving destiny which is far more tempting to the average Christian than fatalism, since it comes cloaked in the appealing garb of theological determinism. This is the belief that everything happens, when and as it happens, because God so wills it. Destiny then means predestination. All events without exception bear on their face the stamp of God's appointing and must therefore be regarded as the outcome of his express command. In such a view fatalism is not answered but only absorbed; it simply becomes a matter of faith.

Now surely it is quite as wrong to want to substitute God for fate as to try to substitute fate for God. This move toward such an identification from the theological side is erroneous for the reason that it makes sheer power central and normative in our conception of God, and power by itself is not God nor even the greater part of God as Jesus Christ reveals him. Furthermore this substitution is downright injurious, as it cuts the nerve of man's responsibility for exactly those attitudes and actions which most plainly show his deep reliance on and confidence in God. It is fortunate indeed that men seldom live by the theories they profess; for if they lived by this dogma of theological determinism, they would very soon cease to live at all. Their best course, as the late Nevin Harner once said, would be to make their way to a quiet room and simply sit, letting God do all the acting and working instead of themselves. Our first step, therefore, in meeting this unwarranted substitution of God for fate must be to give a stout defense of human accountability to God, of human freedom before God.

Such a defense is often undertaken on a purely academic level as the effort to give a rational solution to what appears to be a logical dilemma. Textbooks in ethics or the philosophy of religion usually put this sort of question: "If God wills everything, how can man will anything?" One simply assumes that "will" means the same thing for man and God, that we are faced by contradictory assertions, and must therefore choose between becoming either determinists or libertarians.

But this logical strait-jacketing of the real issue only confuses and thwarts any effort to grapple honestly with it. What is at stake here is not the mere solving of a problem but the understanding of man's actual situation. Need I repeat that here it is a mystery and not a problem that confronts us? For consider how the logical difficulty arises in the first place. Such an issue, posed even in abstractly rational form, emerges in and is concerned with the very meaning of "myself as given"—a meaning which includes my accountability to what is not myself. In short, awareness of my freedom is also awareness of my responsibility. If this were not the case, what point could such a question as the textbooks raise possibly have, what real motivation would impel it, beyond the rather insipid wish to solve a tricky puzzle with verbal sleight of hand?

Without doubt there is a question to be asked about the relation of man's will to that of God, but it does not assume the form of any philosophical parlor game. Instead its shape is utterly and unavoidably existential—that is, it has to do with me. I cannot know myself to be free without also recognizing the limits of my freedom. My freedom is therefore aware of itself, paradoxically perhaps, as unfreedom, and yet without ceasing to be truly free.

For what basically is this much-vaunted freedom of man's will? A clue has already been suggested in the first chapter—that it is self-determination. One wonders whether any sharper, trimmer definition of freedom in this sense has ever been advanced than Jonathan Edwards': "Power to choose and to do what is chosen." Here the conventional restriction of freedom to the power of choice is corrected by a deeper insight, that one cannot really be called free, cannot even be said to choose, unless what he chooses can be carried out or followed through. To be free, then, is to have power, to be able, competent to act. Freedom is the passage from intention to action, bridging both and making one into the other. True, this power is that of deliberating and deciding between equally possible alternatives or courses of action, so that freedom does imply what is often termed an "open future." It is open chiefly in the sense that it is as yet unchosen, yet also in the sense that it is I who must choose rather than the future which must choose me. And let us not forget that freedom of choice is also a certain bondage to choice, for the acceptance of one alternative involves the exclusion of others. Once I have chosen, I am henceforth determined by my choice; as current slang has it, I am "stuck with it." If this were not the case, my very freedom would be no more than a mirage; it could not validate or authenticate itself at all. And again, my competence to choose must also mean ability to act. Deliberation and decision lead on into action, since that is exactly what our intentions do intend. So true is this that even indecision represents a decision in which one chooses not to choose. Thus power to choose and to do what is chosen is what human free will means.

All this may seem pretty elementary to some, but it remains the indispensable starting point for thinking these things through afresh. The same idea of freedom, which is the classical Christian one, is heartily supported by psychoanalysis and psychotherapy in our own day. The way in which they throw light upon this point has been ably summarized by David E. Roberts, who writes:

> The self is not merely the passive resultant of inherited constitution plus environmental influences; it builds up an internal unity of its own which enters actively as well as passively into interplay with the surrounding world and other persons. Yet the character-structure being what it is at a given moment, the thoughts, feelings and actions of that moment follow necessarily. This does not imply that the character-structure cannot change, radically and fundamentally; but it does imply that such changes are "law-abiding" in the sense that they come about in response to specific conditions. . . . Psychotherapy is one version of modern psychology which cannot get along without the "psyche." It sees physical, biological and unconscious processes as participating in the life of a self which is held together, in the end, by consciousness and purposiveness.[1]

We have already seen Paul Tillich making the same point. Freedom to choose and to act in the light of that choice must be, when all is said, freedom to become a self, an "internal unity" or "centered totality" which is both character and author at each stage of life. This particular analogy, in fact, is quite illuminating: the self is very like an author-turned-character in his own play, or

[1] *Psychotherapy and a Christian View of Man* (New York: Chas. Scribner's Sons, 1950), pp. 94, 95. Used by permission of the publisher.

perhaps like a character so thoroughly imbued and involved in the play that he takes on a great deal of the responsibility—though none of the omniscience—of his own author. Selfhood or freedom has then both a passive and an active role, both an originating and a receiving function, each of which imparts its nature to the other.

Freedom means selfhood, then, but there is also a wider meaning than this controlling unity displayed by active potency or competent intention. In order to choose and act as a self, I must do so with reference to my own past choices and actions as well as to the future that lies before me, not to mention those other centers of freedom also known as selves which, as we say, have "wills of their own." To be free therefore is to know and respect the limits of my freedom—those limits which are at once obstacles and opportunities for my own power to choose and act.

May we stay with this rather paradoxical thought a little longer? In order for my freedom to be effective, that is, to *be* freedom, I must accept and work within the conditions of that freedom. Here we return to Tillich's contrast between freedom and destiny—his word for the totality of these conditions at a given moment. The point, I believe, can be made even clearer. Several decades ago in his monumental and moving book on ethics Nicolai Hartmann of Berlin laid down a sort of law—that while lower values exist for the sake of realizing the higher, the higher are nevertheless built upon the lower. Sometimes we illustrate this principle by saying that although man does not live by bread alone, without bread he cannot live at all. Or I may say, quoting the New Testament, that the letter killeth but the spirit giveth life; yet I have not thereby gotten rid of the letter, for to what does the spirit give life if not to the letter? Or again, remember that spiritual communion between persons depends upon physical contact. I am certainly free to visit a friend; yet in order to effect this rather simple purpose, I must make use of bodily automatisms and reflexes, muscular co-ordination, nervous energy, and what not, all of which it would probably take a scientist's lifetime to enumerate in full. The freely purposeful requires the naturally causal not as supplement but as structure, for the very sake of being itself. Thus I can act freely only by acting upon what is not free, bending myself partly into its shape, accepting its conditions in a compliance or willing self-surrender. To come to the point, my very freedom demands of me a certain consent to the conditioning of freedom; and if I do not so consent, I cease to be free.

The body affords a good example of this paradox of freedom-unfreedom; time, as we shall see in the following chapter, provides another. It is far too simple and misleading to assert that my past is determined while my future is free. True, the past is over and done with; yet it is perpetually being refocused and restructured in each present moment, hence continuously renewed and actually changed. This is only to admit that it is *my* past and not another's. And by the same token the future which appears to stretch out trackless and uncharted before me is not at all a realm of pure randomness or chanciness, since it actually puts in front of me some quite specific goals and objects. I do not bring into being the alternatives between which I may choose, no matter how much I help to shape and mold them. Even choice itself, the moment of freedom par excellence, is forever marked by such a complication and consent. We would avoid a great amount of semantic confusion and intellectual chaos if we could stop thinking of freedom as "doing whatever you want." A large part of freedom is precisely this conditionedness of freedom—bodily, temporal, social, causal, and the rest.

The same paradoxical situation is faced on what we call the moral plane, and still more consciously. Here is Paul the apostle again, brooding over the boundary of his freedom: "I do not understand my own actions. For I do not do what I want, but I do the

very thing I hate. . . . I can will what is right, but I cannot do it.
For I do not do the good I want, but the evil I do not want is what
I do." (Rom. 7:15, 18-19.) He not merely is admitting that he has
good intentions but is unable to carry them out; he is making the
far more disturbing admission that he does the very thing he would
not do "for the world." His difficulty then is not that of an in-
sufficient goodness, of a regrettable lack of proportion between intention and action; Paul is not Hamlet "sicklied o'er with the pale
cast of thought" and wavering irresolutely in the face of what he
knows he has to do. No, Paul's difficulty is brought on by having too
much freedom of the wrong kind which blocks and deflects the good
he really wants to do. His very freedom therefore becomes unfree
—incompetent and thwarted—by the presence of a new dimension,
namely, that of sin. And to Paul sin is freedom working as unfreedom, as in fact the self-destruction of freedom.

On the moral plane the conditionedness of freedom becomes
something more terrible and perverse—the self-contradiction of
freedom. That is the meaning Paul gives to sin. It is true that Paul
in some passages seems to externalize sin or at least to partialize it;
sin, he writes, lies in wait, works in us or dwells in us, as if it came
from beyond. But this never constitutes in Paul's eyes an apology
or excuse for sinning. He does not make sin into something that
could not possibly have been different, but he acknowledges that
he is all the more responsible for doing what he cannot avoid. Has
he not allowed it to move in and take possession of his freedom,
turning it instead into slavery? For it is he, Paul, who does both
what he wants and what he hates; the latter, sin, is every bit as
free an action as the former. Yet sin means the abuse of freedom,
not its rightful exercise. It means that freedom has gone wrong, has
signed itself away, has given up the battle.

Let us stay on the track of this thought long enough to note
that sin, however unfree, remains *au fond* the expression of my free-

dom. I am responsible for both using and abusing freedom, which is but to repeat that I cannot abuse it without using it too, but wrongly and perversely. Perhaps this is what the word "willful" basically means—not simply stubborn, but froward and contumacious. The worst, invariably, is the corruption of the best. All this involves that even in sinning I remain strangely free—I am my own man, a real self. No matter what I do, it is still I who do it, I who ought to have done otherwise, I who must live with what I have done. Is this perhaps what Emil Brunner means when in speaking of freedom as self-contradiction he says, "Every man is his own Adam"?

The account I have been giving of freedom may appear to take away with one hand what it pretends to give with the other. Nothing could be further from the truth, however. Accepting Edwards' definition of freedom as our own, we have been testing it out upon the levels of causal condition and moral contradiction. We have seen that it is very far from being what Descartes called a "clear and distinct idea"—it is, rather, a highly tortuous and involved one. And just now, in speaking of sin, it has been found necessary to distinguish between the use and the abuse of freedom. In effect this is to make a distinction between a true and a false freedom, as Augustine marked off "freedom to sin" from "freedom not to sin" many centuries ago.

Do we not find ourselves asking the same question which Paul raised: "Who shall deliver me from this body of death?" In this our life is it possible to be genuinely and gloriously free in the sense that one can do what he really wants to do—the good? And what, moreover, is the vital factor making this difference, which speaking in dead earnest makes all the difference in the world? In the rest of this chapter I shall be suggesting an answer in terms of Providence as the stay and support of our true freedom.

II

There are three Latin phrases which help us to spell out this answer. They are: *Deo volente,* or God willing; *Deo juvante,* or God assisting; and *Deo favente,* or God approving. Each one manages to convey the meaning of that rapport between human willing and the will of God which was referred to earlier, but in a more concrete and positive manner. Let us note them in this order.

The expression "God willing" has obviously a conditional force. We use it to indicate the precarious and uncertain upshot of our human plans and projects. First of all, "God willing" means something like "if what I now expect can be effective in the future" or "if my present purpose is successfully accomplished." The weight of this phrase, as it is commonly employed, is thus upon the "iffy" character of everything my freedom has a hand in making happen. It is my acknowledgment of the contingencies of life, expressing in word if not in deed that "there's many a slip 'twixt the cup and the lip" and that "nothing is certain but death and taxes." By this phrase I grant the large part played by accident and circumstance in hindering or helping my freely chosen lines of action.

And it is well that I should make such an admission, not simply for the sake of steeling myself against possible diappointment later on, but for the purpose of keeping properly humble now. We forget sometimes that a certain degree of agnostic deference and stoical resolve is altogether compatible with Christian living and may even on occasion be required by it. Thus the businessman's new venture which started out so splendidly may turn out to be an utter waste of his time and money. Or the farmer's crop of potatoes may be completely ruined by excessive drought. Or the marriage that begins with parental blessing and personal promise may wind up on the rocks of separation or divorce. Yes, in all things mortal we are menaced by hazard, nonfulfillment, and frustration. By this "God willing," therefore, we express as is quite fitting the inescapable "iffiness" of our existence; we but voice again the ambiguity and anxiety that cling generally to human life.

But we also mean something more in adopting this phrase, namely, that the course of life on earth is ultimately to be referred to God. If we did not mean this, we should rather say, "If chance allows," or, "If luck will have it so." Really, when you think at all carefully about the matter, chance or luck can hardly be supposed to allow anything. For allowance must mean someone's will or nothing, and a bare fortuitousness is the exact opposite of will. So "God willing" means "God permitting"—and if we do not mean this, we had better stop saying it altogether. As Plato long ago made clear, either we believe that God has actual, active power to direct our human steps or else we do not believe in God at all. A do-nothing God is no God, not even a reasonable facsimile thereof.

Yet this permissive power of God we do not regard as coercive. It is not the cause to which our wills are but effects. It does not make us do things, but only gives them leave to happen, gives them room and scope for becoming real. I shall follow up this thought presently.

Now, however, look a bit more steadily at this phrase, as if you actually meant it when you said it. Does it not involve believing that unless God were to allow the outcome that is wished for, it would not in fact occur? For if God permits something to happen, then it must also be true that he does not have to do so but might instead refuse his permission. By allowing it, he thereby holds back something of his power, or perhaps confers that power upon human free will acting as his agent in the world. But in either case I am saying that the determining initiative rests with God.

This point, I think, is of capital importance because we not infrequently refer to God's permission—at least in certain theological circles—as if the term were designed to safeguard human freedom from unwelcome divine interference. To some the idea seems attractive because it appears to give man freer play by reducing God, as it were, to a benevolent shadow of his former self. But our "God willing" does not merely add to an unblushing humanism the old-world patina of an unctuous piety. It is not a device for verbally limiting God or keeping him from getting too much in man's own way. Rather, it is a way of marking off the limits of *our* competence to decide and act. This phrase does far more than to parrot the motto that God helps those who help themselves. Instead it is a homely, honest expression of the deep-rooted Christian conviction that without God our works are vain and our wills are sick. Neither a panicky afterthought nor a deferential nod in the direction of the good Lord, this embodies the very positive belief that the entire condition, context, and consequence of human effort depends finally upon God alone. The stress is throughout on the primary and prior right of God's will over and above the wills of men and women in his world.

Yet we should walk rather warily here. There is no need to overstate the case. The matter of one's perspective is always immensely important in determining what one actually means to say. The divine permission does leave room for man, does give man a chance—his chance—making it possible for us to act either for or against God. In fact, the chief merit of this particular idea in Christian thought is that it suggests so well how God relates himself, both positively and purposefully, to our own freedom. In one of the few solid treatments of Providence in two thousand years of theology, John of Damascus declared that two things are certain: first, that God wills only what is good, since goodness alone belongs to him; second, that we are entirely responsible for our actions and cannot rightly lay them at the door of Providence. Above all else, the doctrine of divine permission is the theological effort to hold these truths together, recognizing that if either is lost sight of, the other is at once deprived of both force and sense.

Plainly enough, a great deal in existence is not good, at all events from the vantage point of human self-fulfillment; and it therefore becomes difficult to believe that God should intend the evil that is so obtrusive in the world. And it is equally clear that we do many things which we cannot seem to help doing, which makes us wonder not unnaturally whether we can be held responsible for them. Now permission is by no means a blanket term invented theologically to cover what is evil in the world and involuntary in ourselves—although we may as well admit that it has been used with just that sort of dodge in mind.

Our Christian understanding is precisely the opposite of that put forward by Max Stirner, a nineteenth-century anarchist who wrote: "Freedom cannot be granted. It must be taken." The Christian believer, on the contrary, must always know and use his freedom as that which has been granted or allowed him. It is the standing witness of that stewardship or trust of which the Gospels speak so often. The same point was put by Thomas Aquinas: "God, by moving voluntary causes, does not deprive their actions of being voluntary, but is rather the cause of this very thing in them." [2] What is underscored here is the truth that human freedom implies, nay, demands, God's freedom; so that when it is most itself, it is also most his.

Again, in holding that God permits evil to occur we are not thereby saying that he is helpless or powerless in the face of evil. Obviously, if God had simply to confront evil as brute fact, he would not in any reasonable sense be allowing it to be; he would merely be acknowledging its greater power over against himself. Once more, permission always means something very like volition and

[2] *Summa Theologica,* Ia, question 83, art. 1.

consent. With respect to evil this involves that God may well have purposes of his own which no mortal mind can fathom. And with reference to freedom the divine permission means quite precisely that our wills are willed by God, however badly they may express themselves in wrong choices and sinful motives.

I do not think we clarify this matter either by rejecting out of hand the whole idea of divine permission, like Emil Brunner, or by making nice intramural distinctions within the will of God, like Leslie Weatherhead and Nels Ferré. In the former case the idea which has been rejected comes sneaking back in everything but name under the heading of the divine self-limitation. In the latter the conception of divine permission, "purposive but not intentional," becomes so complicated and overextended that every vestige of real permissiveness disappears from it. What God wills, he wills; and since he is one, his will must be also one. Little is gained for either faith or reason by distinguishing modes of theoretical intentionality within God's will. Then it is difficult to avoid giving the impression that one knows more about God's inner constitution than God does himself.

As we deal with such issues as these, we ought, I believe, to keep our keenest and most existential questions to the fore, since it is there that our initial reason for speaking of God's permission lies. Why do I do the things I shouldn't? How can I be responsible for what I can't help? Why don't things come out the way I plan or want them? These, indeed, are boundary situations which force us well out toward the limit of our own wills, where the further question of God's will is suddenly pertinent, and yet also where any attempt to diagram God must seem quite out of place.

To repeat, the doctrine of divine permission is not a rational device for giving a so-called "explanation" of the presence of sin and evil in the world. Instead, it means to say that God is both great and good enough to be permissive with respect to his creation. He reveals his power and purpose not alone by causing things to be but also by letting things happen which he might indeed prevent. God in his own freedom allows his creatures to be free—free to do evil as well as good, to make our own mistakes, to test our powers upon the real world order. As Scripture says, God has already in his good pleasure allowed us to will and to do; and we may here add Dante's word, that in his will is our peace. Far, then, from limiting God or bifurcating God, this doctrine safeguards his unity and sovereignty by placing all things under Providence. Without wishing to remove the fundamental mystery of existence, the doctrine reaffirms that it is all within God's keeping and concern.

III

What now of *Deo juvante,* "God assisting"? This expression is not as common as the first, but what is meant by it is equally familiar in our Christian outlook. Theologians of the patristic and scholastic periods called this meaning the doctrine of divine cooperation or concurrence. Quite recently there has been a reaction, understandably sharp, to this way of putting Providence. It may even be the case that our current Protestant failure to take Providence with full seriousness theologically is bound up with an inherited aversion to this particular idea. Some will not conceive God as assisting man because such a thought seems to dethrone him, making him no more than an assistant or fellow worker. They ask whether a God who only helps man out is not too much a God "down in the dirt," as William James pictured him. How can he possibly be the God of Abraham, Isaac, and Jacob, the high and holy one who inhabits eternity?

But this again depends upon the perspective from which these faith-statements are made. What if this view of the divine concurrence, like that of the divine permission, turns out to be an enlargement and not a diminution of our Protestant witness? Not even the most intransigent defender of neo-orthodoxy would wish to expurgate from the Bible the many passages in which God is approached or addressed as the support or stay of man. How could he do so and still lay claim to being a Christian believer?

Let us say at once that to maintain that God assists man does not make him into a mere assistant, as if that were everything we knew about God. Instead it is to raise the glad, surprised, undying testimony that he is our very present help in trouble, that he alone makes us to dwell in safety and is at our right hand evermore. Nothing should prevent us from joining in this grateful witness today, when so many cheap and banal substitutes for Providence are being offered. And no theological partisanship, in particular, should keep us from thinking through its Christian meaning, since after all the doctrine of Providence is only a kind of theological praise.

Among contemporary Christian thinkers none has put the case for belief in Providence more effectively than Herbert H. Farmer of Cambridge. He has wisely written that the Christian meets God both as absolute demand and as final succor, and in this vein he continues:

The unconditional demands, the values of God, are apprehended as pointing the way to the highest self-realization, the final security of man. The divine will resists and sets a limit to our personal desires and preferences of a peculiarly absolute kind; none the less it can be trustfully obeyed, for it is in the same world of values with ourselves, or rather it is the ultimate foundation of it. In its very resistance, therefore, it is, in a unique and ultimate way, co-operative. . . . To know God livingly and fully as personal He must be apprehended at one and the same time as "consuming fire" and as "refuge and strength." It is an idle question to ask why this should be the manner of God's self-disclosure to the soul of man. The necessity lies in the character of God Himself, and in that order of personal relations, of relations between personal wills, which springs from Him. It is given in the original

73

unity of the universe, inherent in which is the primordial *rapport* between man and God, and God and man.[3]

I would, I think, be quite shortsighted to let our present theological distaste for words such as "values" and "self-realization" obscure the real point Farmer is making. There *is* a close relationship in our Christian faith between demand and succor, justice and mercy; and these not simply are antithetical assertions about God which constitute a kind of logical riddle, but symbolize as well as human words can the manifold action of the one Lord and Father. Hence the task of any theologian in articulating and ordering the truth of faith is not to balance these against each other in a synthetic way, but rather to show how each involves and means the other. We do not have to make a rational choice between a God who demands and a God who helps. Rather, we have to choose both; otherwise we shall have neither. Only if God has ultimate power of his own, can he be truly regarded as the helper of man; and only if he is our helper, can we properly worship him as Lord. One chief merit of the doctrine of Providence is that it must refuse to accept this Marcionistic posing of alternative gods, but insists that both universal concern and ultimate control belong to the one true God.

This may appear to be something of a digression, yet it is actually central to the present variation on the theme of Providence. For one thing, it should be seen immediately that to believe in the divine concurrence or assistance means that man stands in dire need of such help and indeed cannot go on without it. The basis of the doctrine in experience is always that man needs God and finds him answering that need with power and love. To be sure, we may not invariably discover God at the exact moment of our need; and we

[3] *The World and God* (New York: Harper & Bros., 1936), pp. 25, 26. Used by permission of the publisher.

may be more acutely conscious of our need at some times than at others. Still, the confident refrain of believers in all generations is that "the Lord is my strength and my shield; my heart trusted in him, and I am helped." (Ps. 28:7).

Instead, then, of pushing the eternal God far out toward the periphery of man's view of things, this doctrine of divine co-operation finds God to be crucially involved in every good work man can do. Not that God runs alongside man *pari passu,* with equal step, a little out of breath perhaps, letting man take the lead while he plays only a supporting role. An adequate faith in the incarnate and redeeming Lord would here do much to mitigate our reluctance to see God as our coworker and companion. Because of Jesus Christ the trust in God as "very present help" becomes a living, permanent force in human life. God may well be infinitely more than that, but certainly no less. It is our faith that God's help is forever contrapuntal to man's lack and need.

What must be avoided, of course, in any statement of this faith is the false and Pharisaical perspective which takes God entirely too much for granted, since it looks to him as merely the underwriter, guarantor, or backer of our human plans and plots and pleasures. For any overestimation of man's capacity for virtue, with the consequent underestimation of man's liability to sin, cannot from the beginning realize that it is actually God who comes, as he will surely come, to our aid. This throws a very different light upon the *Deo juvante* than either Pelagianism or even Molinism can possibly cast. God is the author and finisher of human good, not our auxiliary and certainly not our accomplice.

Secondly, this old, neglected doctrine of co-operation means that man, in order to bring his works to a good and right end, requires the assistance of God. A prayer by E. B. Pusey, one of the leaders in the Oxford Movement a century ago, makes this particularly clear: "Enable me to commend myself in all things to Thee;

grant me in all things to please Thee; bring me through all things nearer unto Thee." Here there is no question of making some sort of technical adjustment to God or of tapping the divine resource for reasons of one's own. On the contrary, it is a question of serving God, not using him. The truth is that man's goodness is really his need of God and fits into the divine help like a hand placed within a larger, stronger hand. Providence as the divine concurrence is emphatically not the belief that nothing succeeds like success or that God adds his surplus power to our already demonstrated effectiveness. It rather signifies that out of weakness we are made strong, not out of strength made even stronger. In other words, our relationship to God is necessarily an asymmetrical one and not a junior partnership within a common enterprise.

The doctrine of concurrence is closely analogous to that of the divine conservation with respect to the natural world—although to draw this parallel carefully would take us quite beyond the scope of this book. It may, however, be mentioned in passing that the Greek fathers, for example, often use these terms interchangeably. So Gregory Nazianzen speaks of God conserving what he has created by declaring that nothing can survive in nature, especially human beings, without the ever-present "concurrence" of God. Likewise Origen tries to compare Providence in the universe to a well-ordered house arranged by human foresight and prudence. So too John of Damascus, who has been already cited, moves with considerable ease from nature to the moral life and back again, saying that as we cannot add anything to our height, so it is God's providence that brings each work of ours that is good to execution. Without Providence, therefore, no cares, pains, efforts, on our part could be of any possible value. That is the major stress in these ancient doctrines of concurrence, which makes some of the conventional Protestant strictures seem very wide of the mark.

But we may be more specific and positive. This understanding that God assists men, like that of the divine permission, has to do with the rapport, as Farmer called it in the passage quoted earlier, between human wills and the will of God himself. As permission, however, is connected with man's sin, so concurrence has primarily in view man's good works. It gives theological statement to the truth of faith that while man by himself does evil, only God can be the author and finisher of whatever good man may accomplish. The same truth may be put in moral terms: I know myself to be responsible—not merely held responsible—for the evil I do, as for the good I leave undone. That is, I can find no honorable way of putting the blame for my wrongdoing upon God. But quite as plainly, I cannot congratulate myself on the good things I do, since I know that I am not solely responsible for them. I must therefore regard God as at least the coauthor of these fugitive and scattered good works of mine. And thus the heart of the matter, speaking morally, is just this acceptance of personal responsibility for evil done or good undone, together with this refusal to take credit for good done or evil turned to good account. All this is by virtue of the faith that God, who does not connive with us in the wrong use of our freedom, nevertheless brings into fulfillment by his strength working in us whatever good is humanly realized.

For even as God does not relieve us of accountability for our actions, so he does not abandon us completely to our own devices. Yes, all things are possible with God—even the good we are able to do. This way of thinking, obviously, avoids the near-blasphemy hinted in the statement that "God has no hands but our hands." Moreover it puts the accent rightly by insisting that our working and our willing must be conformed to God's. One might almost say that this doctrine of concurrence is the theological mode of Fénelon's devotional principle "Let God act." To repeat: this is by no means a nice alignment of my will with that of God, but a making way for God, a putting of myself at God's disposal. Far more than any sort of adjustment, my free will must make a total personal response of yielding or surrender in order for the good to be done. Let me put it like this: I am called upon to co-operate with God, not in the sense of doing what God cannot do without me, but in the sense of doing what I cannot do without God.

Thus it follows, once again, that Providence is not a causal or even a pseudo-causal explanation of my freedom. If it were, our freedom would not in fact be free and Providence would be anything but providential. Rather, Providence means God's freedom acting creatingly and savingly upon our own, permitting evil, to be sure, but just as surely inspiring and effecting good. And so our freedom is not less free because it is God's gift to us, but more so, since it is by that token infinitely more responsible.

A final word on this teaching with regard to the divine assistance concerns its pertinence right now. What makes it presently so valuable is that it points toward that which is truly salvable in man without either minimizing the radical grip of sin upon us or landing in the pitfalls of moralism and activism. It means that there is that in man, even at his fallen worst, which enables him to cast himself on God and to give over his life into the divine keeping. If the twenty-third psalm could be rendered in theological prose, it would sound very much like this doctrine I have been expounding.

And the doctrine means still more, namely, that there is that in God which is forever ready to restore man's freedom to its authentic level from the bondage into which we have plunged ourselves, working in us not only repentance but also renewal. Thus the misery of man without God becomes the grandeur of man with God. As Thomas Aquinas wrote, the divine will works *suaviter et fortiter,* sweetly and strongly, in the heart of man, sowing the divine seed and presiding watchfully over its growth. This note has been rather conspicuously absent in recent Protestant thinking, but it must be recovered if we are to realize afresh the glorious liberty of the sons of God.

IV

And so we come to the third phrase in this glossary of Providence, *Deo favente,* or "God approving." This brings into view the whole dimension of the grace of God. In reality I have been talking about grace all through this chapter, as the doctrines of freedom, permission, and concurrence presuppose and embody it. God can neither assist nor allow unless he favors us. Even wrath and punishment, not to mention sin and evil, are classically understood by Christians as God's grace withheld or withdrawn. Certainly a gracious disposition on the part of God toward men is basic wherever Christians believe, love, or hope.

But this thought needs to be made clearer. What can be more relevant, for example, to a pastor's counseling of people in distress than the affirmation of the grace of God? The same may be said for teaching and preaching in the churches. All these activities, so normal and constant in the Christian ministry, would be greatly strengthened by a firmer grasp upon this whole range of truth concerning God's way with man.

Now the idea that God takes something like a personal interest in human affairs, approving or disapproving their course and favoring some actions over others, is not exclusively Christian but belongs generally to the religious consciousness. To take but one example, Plato defended this in the tenth book of the Laws, and of course the Old Testament abounds in illustrations of the same belief. Yet in our own faith grace is centered in a unique way in the lordship of Christ, which is most revealing theologically. We may even agree with Thomas F. Torrance in saying:

Grace in the New Testament is the basic and the most characteristic element of the Christian Gospel. It is the breaking into the world of the ineffable love of God in a deed of absolutely decisive significance which cuts across the whole of human life and sets it on a new basis. That is actualised in the person of Jesus Christ, with which grace is inseparably associated, and supremely exhibited on the Cross by which the believer is once and for all put in the right with God. This intervention of God in the world and its sin, out of sheer love, and His personal presence to men through Jesus Christ are held together in the one thought of grace.[4]

The sort of discussion of grace which is reflected in these words of Torrance has been carried on chiefly in the context of our rediscovery of Paul's view of faith as radical and obedient response to God's own self-disclosure in Christ. It has become characteristic in this neo-Paulinism to think of grace as a kind of counterpart to faith, the secret of faith, in fact the sole, sufficient occasion of faith.

Although we may rejoice that grace has been so much emphasized in present-day theology, we also have cause to regret that it has frequently been set forth in the per-emptory tone of the above passage. It might, I think, not unfairly be said that while we have without doubt been recovering the sense of the gratuitous element in God's grace, we have not become aware in like degree of what is after all supremely gracious about it.

It is of course plain that grace is forever gratuitous; in Charles Péguy's words, "it twists and turns and is full of surprises." No rendering of grace, therefore, in terms which suggest that it can be manipulated or managed from the human end can begin to do justice to what the word itself means. For grace is but another way of saying that God is utterly and sovereignly free. It means his own right to be God. That Christian thought has often distorted if not

[4] *The Doctrine of Grace in the Apostolic Fathers* (Edinburgh: Oliver & Boyd, Ltd., 1948), p. 34. Used by permission of the publisher.

destroyed the very meaning it has tried to expound is true and has to be admitted and regretted. Grace, precisely in order to be grace, must be gratuitous—that is, spontaneous, uncalled for, undeserved, and uncontrollable by will or work of men. A Christian takes his stand on that.

And yet there is something different which also must be said. To say that grace is gracious, too, may seem at first glance to be almost ridiculously obvious. It must be stressed, however, for the reason that it often goes unsaid today. The great slogans of the Reformation, *sola gratia, sola fide,* have brought home to us the inescapable mysteriousness of Christian living, indeed the utter dependence of man upon God for everything he has and is and may become. All this is very much to the point, but in more recent versions of our faith there has been a dropped accent, a forgotten factor. The missing element is just that spirit of wondering gratitude which is always the genuine Christian response to the action of an altogether gracious God. It is as if we had been analyzing grace without ever really becoming acquainted with it. Perhaps we have gotten so much in the habit of being told what grace is not that we now need to be reminded of what grace actually is.

When the action of God upon the human soul is pictured as an "encounter" or "confrontation" or "intervention," we are using for the purpose metaphors which are cold and spatial rather than warm and temporal, impersonal rather than personal. Such analogies underscore up-againstness, not communion or participation. Almost inevitably, therefore, they tend to leave us with the impression that grace is God's free *act* without being also God's free *gift*. This may not be intended so much as inadvertent, yet the impression remains. For example, does not Torrance's description of grace have this effect? Grace, he writes, is a "breaking into" or a "cutting across" and not an indwelling or a taking up. In such a view Christ is more

81

like a meteor flashing down out of a dark sky than the Word who dwells with us in fullness of grace.

It is probably not so much a matter of untruth in what is being said as of the truth which is being left unsaid. These images, when spelled out into a system, do indeed keep sharp and clean the line between what God does and what man can do; and that is most important. But from this it need not follow at all that human action is totally vain or fruitless, still less that from God's point of view there is no worth or merit in a believing, loving, hoping kind of life. This distinction, however salutary for thought, has no right to impose itself as a disruption within existence itself. For if the Christian knows anything, he knows that he is not merely "intersected" or "invaded" by the grace of God, but rather initiated and incorporated into grace. What real difference does the "grace of our Lord Jesus Christ" make to us unless it becomes structured in character and operative in conduct here below?

We may sharpen the issue if we return briefly to Torrance's account of grace in the apostolic fathers. He complains that they related grace "to the continuance of the Christian life, rather than to the decisive motion of God's love as the presupposition of the whole Christian life." [5] He warns against allowing grace to become, as he claims it often did in the subsequent thinking of the church, a mere *donum superadditum,* that is, an extra gift of surplus goodness which is then auxiliary to man's sanctification. But surely we do not have to excuse such a regrettable tendency in order to point out that there is a surprising lack in Torrance's own understanding of grace—the conviction, namely, that what God gives he gives for our good as well as for his own glory, and that his love is fully gracious no less than utterly gratuitous, and further that this means the empowering and lifting up of all our life. Granted that God's

[5] *Ibid.,* p. 139.

love must be the presupposition of our faith, must it not also be the predisposition of his grace?

Yes, we deeply need to recover our theological balance on this matter of grace. The alternative to Torrance's "interventionism" is not a bland inclusiveness which regards grace as a sort of perpetual smile on God's face, like the stony, insufferable smile on the angel carved into the portal of Rheims Cathedral. The doctrine of grace is not our happy Christian answer to the question, Is the universe friendly? No, it is the statement of our inalienable conviction that, in the words of a hymn by Isaac Watts:

> Supreme in wisdom as in power
>   The Rock of Ages stands;
> Though Him thou canst not see, nor trace
>   The working of His hands.
>
> He gives the conquest to the weak,
>   Supports the fainting heart;
> And courage in the evil hour
>   His heavenly aids impart.

Or if you should prefer a more laconic, up-to-date expression, there is Robert Frost's "You can't trust God to be unmerciful."

This is not a treatise on the doctrine of grace; but if it were, we should want to insist upon and demonstrate the force of the graciousness of God as it is disclosed, nay, embodied, in Jesus Christ our Lord. Yet here our point must be a more restricted one, concerning as it does the connection between grace and Providence. Fundamental to any setting forth of Providence is the truth that God's sovereignty or primacy with reference to human willing is gracious as well as gratuitous, that his initiative is not only the presupposition of Christian thought but even more the loving predisposition felt and relied upon in Christian experience, and that apart from grace in this sense there can be no real grasp of the nature of Providence. While we may not wish to go as far as Karl Barth, who identifies the two, we must always see the one as illumined by the other, else we cannot rightly understand either Providence or grace.

I shall conclude this chapter, therefore, with a strong restatement of the way in which God's grace—that is, his freedom to act and to give—bears in upon man's own use of freedom—that is, his right to be a self and to achieve his purposes in earthly life. It is by God's grace that I am permitted to exist at all and by his grace that I may truly co-operate with him. And when I am not helped by grace to do the things I should, the reason is not in God but in myself. So whatever good I may attain is by God's approval; this, moreover, is not merely a nod from on high but an empowering transformation working and willing in me by the same mighty love that was made forever plain in Jesus. Yet I do not stop being myself when I do the will of God. I do not, as Simone Weil recommends, "de-create" myself. It is not that my own will retires while God's will occupies the space left empty. The vitality and spontaneity of my own freedom still find full expression. "I live; yet not I," wrote Paul; and this may be transcribed theologically by saying that God's grace transforms itself into the motive power of my freedom, not by breaking personal integrity but by enhancing and releasing it. There are not two actions, God's and mine, but rather one, my own made good by grace. This was the point of the citation given earlier from Thomas Aquinas, that by moving the will God does not deprive it of freedom but really makes it free as it could never have been by itself.

If this seems paradoxical, we shall have to make the most of it. In any case it is the repeated testimony of Christian experience. The rather dry words of theology form, as it were, the skeletal structure of the living body of a faithful response. God's grace may well come in the first instance as an intrusion or invasion from beyond our freedom, but the fully surrendered will knows its true worth and weight as grace becomes ingredient within that will's own momentum and operation. Again and again Christians have joyously confessed, not that they were taken over or manipulated by God, but that they *found themselves* in him. This real experience needs to be interpreted with fidelity and care. To say, "For to me to live is Christ," is more than anything else to understand the very meaning of my life. It is to become branch to vine, member to body; to be taken up and made participant in God's ongoing, inward purpose. "The way of man is not in himself," said Jeremiah; this is to say that insofar as God makes himself our companion and co-worker, and only so, can we become his. This is the true meaning of the doctrine of grace as it throws light upon the pilgrimage of faith, and it is the meaning of the doctrine of Providence as well.

In creed and cult and conduct let it be eagerly voiced that the Lord our God is gracious, slow to anger, and plenteous in mercy. It is through Jesus Christ our Lord that we have the right to believe this. Through him whose surrender was the surest mark of his sovereignty we can finally understand the quality of God's will as love. And we can see how his freedom modulates and engraces our own, making us free indeed.

Theology may certainly help in finding truer ways of saying all this. And yet one wonders if it can ever finally improve upon the folk wisdom of the Christian life, with its assurance lived and known that although man proposes, God disposes. A man's heart may devise his way, but it is the Lord who directs his steps. And the further one grows into the life in Christ, the truer this becomes. Our faith in Providence is of a piece with that experienced fact. It celebrates the favoring, assisting, leave-giving God—the God in whom and through whom and to whom are all things, the God to whom all glory shall be given forever and ever.

4

The Heart of Time

"Thou art my God. My times are in thy hand."—*Ps. 31:14-15*

There is a heroine in one of Marcel's plays, a witty and attractive woman named Christiane, who is much admired as a hostess and greatly valued as a friend. Her life is seemingly complete and successful; but just beneath the surface there is a suspicion—yes, an anguished emptiness—that breaks through into speech. In one place she says, musingly but with growing fervor:

"Don't you feel sometimes that we are living . . . if you can call it living . . . in a broken world? Yes, broken like a broken watch. The mainspring has stopped working. But put the watch to your ear, and you don't hear any ticking. You know what I'm talking about, the world, what we call the world, the world of human creatures. . . . It seems to me it must have had a heart once, but today you would say the heart has stopped beating." [1]

For how many people, do you suppose, is Christiane here speaking? Although she is but a creature of the playwright's imagination, she is more a symbol than a fiction. Her words, almost casual and yet extremely moving, lay bare a misgiving which is shared by countless folk today whose mode of life can scarcely be called living. Their world, if not already broken, is at least decidedly ques-

[1] From *Le monde cassé,* quoted in Gabriel Marcel, *The Mystery of Being* (Chicago: Henry Regnery Co., 1950), pp. 21-22.

tionable. May we not then recognize in Christiane's reflections that very mistrust of human destiny which the doctrine of Providence is called upon to answer?

I

We do not often put our deepest questions into so frank a form as this, since they lie too far down to be expressed fully and are perhaps too embarrassing to be openly confessed. Usually we make a kind of translation of these queries into a language that is more readily spoken and from which much of their original hurt or ache has been expelled. Rather often, in fact, all that is left of the original question is the sighing inflection or the querulous punctuation in the voice of the speaker.

Among the questions stirring in the place where words come from, there is one suggested by Christiane's own way of speaking. It concerns the nature of time, elusive yet coercive. What really is the import of this peculiarly inconstant constant running through all the variables of our destiny? And what, if anything, does it have to tell us about God?

Clearly, time is not a fact which can be isolated and observed and analyzed. As Augustine once remarked, when nobody asks us what time is, we know; but when we try to explain it, we do not know. Instead of a fact time seems to be a sort of dimension, or perhaps direction, within which every fact is met and measured. It is indeed baffling, as it wears as many faces as the clocks and watches in a jewelry shop. It may creep at a petty pace from day to day or gallop breathlessly by like the Four Horsemen of the Apocalypse. There are moments that seem never to end and whole years that vanish without appearing to leave a single trace. When I have engagements to meet, I fear time as a tyrant; but in moods of calm reflection I may bless time as the healer of my disappointments and resentments. As Shakespeare put it: "Time travels in diverse paces with diverse persons. I'll tell you who Time ambles withal, who Time trots withal, who Time gallops withal, and who he stands still withal." Yes, the oddly shifting tempo of time, its well-nigh contradictory variety, is one of the profoundest riddles of our human pilgrimage.

And yet we may be begging the whole question by calling human life in time a pilgrimage. Actually a large part of Christiane's suspicion is whether life can truly be said to be anything of the sort. For if time is as all-including and perplexing as it appears to be, must not human destiny likewise be unstable and uncertain? A pilgrim is on his way somewhere and knows with some assurance the direction of his going, but can the same be believed and said of men and women insofar as they are creatures of time? Are we really pilgrims, headed somewhere and knowing it, or only wanderers making ignorant circles in the woods of time?

Creatures of time we human beings most indubitably are, but what is the character of that which fashions us? One answer, generally held today, is that time means change, is simply identical with change. In one of the most pregnant sentences coming out of modern philosophy, Henri Bergson wrote, "There are no things that change; there is only change." His words had time very much in mind. And when Augustine said that "time takes no holiday," he expressed the same thought. There are times, all sorts and shapes and sizes; but there is also Time, or Change. May this not be the last word on the matter?

So we are tempted to become quite fatalistic about the nature of temporal change, regarding it as a necessity from which there can be no recourse. Then we may quote Shakespeare on the "dark backward and abysm of time" or Ben Jonson on "that old bald cheater, Time." In this mood time is identified as something to which nothing can be added and from which nothing can be expected. We think that it may even be the force of fate itself, not fixed but moving, always surrounding and surging through us. Repeatedly our tragic intuition tells us that time must be the very momentum of fate, enslaving all events and exempting none. To be sure, there are times we are happy, and other times make us blue; but what does this mean if not that human pain and pleasure are alike effects produced by time as the cause, and quite possibly even the sport of time? It is because of our submergence in changeful time that life seems but "a sleep and a forgetting" in which we are "[carried] . . . away as with a flood" and must "spend our years as a tale that is told."

Does it come with something of a shock to realize that these last two phrases are drawn not from fatalistic literature but from Scripture? The ninetieth psalm, in which they appear, is only one among many places which give proof that the Bible knows as much as any atheist or agnostic about the changeful temporality of our earthly lot. Yes, the Bible yields to no other book in its complete realism about time, holding that time conditions by its restless, relentless movement everything a man has or can do. And Christian hymns reveal the same understanding, as in Isaac Watts's familiar stanza:

> Time, like an ever-rolling stream,
> Bears all its sons away;
> They fly forgotten, as a dream
> Dies at the opening day.

May not our entire existence, when considered from the viewpoint of time, be no pilgrimage at all but "only a dream a little less inconstant" than our dreams themselves? It sobers us to realize that this haunting thought is taken up into the very heart of Christian praise, as if it could not be gainsaid by even the strongest faith. In this respect, indeed, Christianity is at one with the skeptical temper in both Eastern and Western cultures; it does not evade the changeable and precarious aspects of our life but repeatedly affirms them. Yet Christianity does not parrot skepticism in suspecting that living may be only dreaming; although it understands that such a suspicion is made plausible by recognizing as we must that to exist at all is to be forever passing out of one moment into the next, without even knowing when one moment becomes the next. What is common ground for doubter and believer, however, is the awareness that to live means to be continually and mortally in transit, like boats adrift with no sure anchorage or birds of passage with no safe nesting place in reality.

Therefore it is understandable that men should think of time-in-general as something that wears the mask of death, carrying life downstream toward nothingness. But it is actually impossible to live and work as if this thought were true. Do not all of us insist on believing, in spite of strong persuasions to the contrary, that human existence has a permanent significance and leaves some lasting mark upon the real? When he wrote the following words, André Gide was surely speaking for everyone: "I have in myself a great need of permanence—I mean a need of believing that there are products not subject to decay and degradation, works on which temporal changes have no influence." [2] Whoever writes a book, or raises a family, or teaches the young, or builds himself into an institution, must sooner or later confess to that same need. We deeply want what we are doing to be worth while, to last and count for something, to be confirmed and made secure by whatever powers there be. And so like Gide we make this living protest against deathly time, not only when some mainspring in us has stopped working but as each day ticks on toward night.

In the Christian faith, as in the Bible, this protest is transformed into a prayer: "Establish thou the work of our hands upon

[2] *The Journals of André Gide* (New York: Alfred A. Knopf, Inc., 1951), IV, vii.

us; yea, the work of our hands establish thou it." Such a prayer, let it be noted, does not set at naught what Dylan Thomas called the burn and turn of time; and yet it assumes a vantage point which may prove to be of tremendous importance for both thought and life. For in the perspective of our faith God maintains toward all time a relationship that is both positive and providential, so that he is able to keep us from falling away into mere transiency and utter futility. One major task of the doctrine of Providence becomes that of showing just what ground in reason and what relevance to our condition this whole perspective has, through justifying the conviction that time—in spite of Christiane's misgiving—has something like a heart, after all.

II

What is needed, to begin with, is a far more serious grasp of that which is involved in our own experience of time. To be sure, it is difficult for us to keep our thought about time at this human level. All our models for it are mechanical, which encourages us to use technical jargon and to make abstract analyses. Yet this is exactly what we must not do if we are going to answer the question that is raised by omnipresent, all-including time. The focus of our thought must be the human, lived reality of time, which means no more or less than the temporal context and condition of our fears, hopes, hates, loves. It means the unobtrusive but inevitable structuring by time of every nook and cranny of our experience. However, it is our experience that is so structured, which makes time not a wholly unknown quantity and certainly not a problematic x required to complete some metaphysical equation.

And thus the dialectic of our thought begins. Although nothing human is foreign to time, time is plainly not automatically or universally friendly to man. We attempt to capture time and put it to work for us, pinning it down in calendars and clocks. But time is what winds up and runs down every clock, and makes all calendars finally obsolete. At last unmeasurable but always measuring, time is the fugitive accompaniment of our way through life. It is as mysterious as it is ubiquitous. One can hardly help wondering about this fact of time's incomprehensibility. Is it because time is so much a part of us or because we are so much a part of time?

Admittedly I dwell in time. My past is largely reverie, my future mostly riddle. Although I can turn my watch backward or forward at will, time appears to move on with majestic indifference to my convenience and comfort. What is more, it moves in one direction only, from yesterday and toward tomorrow through today. It cannot be reversed or even arrested in its course. I am, it seems, being pushed incessantly out to the moving edge of time; I am made to live in the demanding present when I should prefer to linger in the past or to leap headlong into the future. We wander in the times that are not ours, as Pascal said, but it is time that brings us up short, prodding our efforts even as it threatens our achievements. Yes, the one thing I can never do is to get away from time, but I am not simply frozen by time; instead I am carried along in its current, now slow, now rapid—and who can say where it is taking me?

This is the nature of time-in-general, which in the first gesture of my thought inclines me to identify ceaseless flux as the entire meaning of time itself. For I am constantly being remade by time. It is always bringing me up to date and making me out of date. This double movement, moreover, seems to be at bottom one, since I am carried in one direction only. The very benevolence of time results from this evident relentlessness of its conditioning. To quote Pascal, "Time heals griefs and quarrels, for we change and are no longer the same persons. Neither the offender nor the offended are anymore the same. . . . Our nature consists in motion; complete rest is death." [3] Little wonder, then, that I should see myself as merely one

[3] *Op. cit.,* p. 46.

thing among others, hurried and tumbled along by time, external-
ized, anonymous, herded into line. If even time's benign effects
have their cause in this destroying force, how can I be heartened or
hopeful under its control?

But wait—the second movement of my thought is taking shape
—time is also in me. Is it not a kind of built-in measuring device by
which I take my world in stride, exert my strength, and weave my
web of meaning? By means of time I am able to plan my campaigns,
husband my resources, gather in my harvests. Now my thought is
growing more confident and less despairing: if I am what I am
because of time, may not time be what it is because of me? Although there is always time-in-general to be reckoned with, there
is also time-in-particular—a time to mourn and a time to dance, a
time to get and a time to lose, a time of war and a time of peace.
And so this singular plurality of time, this manyness-in-oneness,
spells far more than servitude and defeat. Time does not require me
to manage all of life at once. If, as the Bible declares, there is a
time for everything under the sun, then I can *take my time,* living
and working in the present that is given to me without nursing
yesterday's regret or prying into tomorrow's secret.

As I go on thinking thus about time, I seem more and more to
come free of its tyranny; for am I not continually remaking time
rather than being remade by it? And may it not be just because
time waits for no man that I can "take the instant by the forward
top?" Now I am putting increased emphasis upon the pliability of
time to creative human self-determination; I am recognizing that it
is not only available but even advantageous to me and my projects.

This, or something like it, would appear to be the human, lived
reality of time—a strange mixture of winning and losing, manage-
ability and menace. From one point of view I am the passive serf
of time, which is precisely what Whitehead called it, a "perpetual
perishing"—sheer successiveness and fateful flux. From another,

time seems on the whole to be quite amenable at least to some of my needs and longings, and then I think with Kierkegaard of "the Moment" which is both opportune and decisive. Time-in-general, coming and going like the tide, and time-in-particular, with its pointed significance for all my striving, both of these belong to our experience and must be reckoned with in its interpretation.

Must we conclude, then, that contradiction has the last word to say on this subject? Is it necessary to take refuge in deliberate paradox in order to communicate the human meaning of time? Without denying that any adequate statement concerning time must have a paradoxical edge to it, since so great a mystery cannot possibly be caught in any man's net, we may at all events affirm that these alternative ways of looking at time do imply and complement each other. I am able to make every minute count only by virtue of the fact that time is carrying me forward in spite of myself. The very possibility of choosing or acting in the present moment is grounded in the necessity of living from what is no longer toward what is not yet. Hence, if time is as inexorable as fate, it is also as irresistible as grace. A rule of thought is clearly emerging here: *time endured is the condition of time enjoyed*. Or to put the same truth differently, each time-in-particular is grounded in the nature of time-in-general; so that the decisive value of today proceeds from the fact that tomorrow is already crowding the horizon and that yesterday has already receded from the scope of human powers.

> But at my back I always hear
> Time's wingèd chariot hurrying near.

Yet more remains to be said, for any account that claims to be true must include the character of time as plastic and amenable to human purposes. It can be adapted to our own requirements and provides us with many undeniable resources. Whatever it is "out there," apart from us, time cannot be truly understood without giving due weight to the fact that it assists and furthers us in many ways. If time-in-particular is grounded in time-in-general, it also must be said that time-in-general is expressed only through specific moments as they come into existence. We are not simply thrown into a losing race with time; and victory is not necessarily to the strong or the swift, for the hare may have to yield to the tortoise. This old fable, in fact, means that time is not all of a piece but comes fitted as it were to our capacities and shares in their diversity.

True, time means perpetual perishing, but only because it also means perpetual renewing. If the present moment is forever vanishing, then it must be always there to vanish. May not time be fed by secret springs of which, perhaps, it is the ignorant token? A second rule of thought is coming to the fore: *every Now is really new,* or else its very "nowness" is a bald-faced lie. Precisely in the compulsiveness of time consists its creativeness. It is actually time's way of pushing me ahead of myself that makes it possible for me to find in it my sphere of freedom.

These two rules must be thought together, as the realities for which they stand are lived together. In attempting to maintain this equilibrium, we need to guard against misunderstandings which threaten us from opposite sides. The first is a view of time which still persists in some quarters, though it has been pretty thoroughly discredited in others. This is the notion that time means progress; a good symbol for it might be the department-store escalator which carries customers from a lower to a higher floor if only they will get on and ride. According to it every tragedy is but a temporary setback, human sin is merely cultural lag, and man's direction in time is inevitably onward and upward. In this myopic view all past ages are judged and found wanting by one's own, which constitutes the highest level yet attained.

It is by no means easy to believe in such a view today, when almost all our cultural values have had to be so drastically revalued, and when what looked like progress now seems in the light of its consequences to be anything but progress. Furthermore, this view disintegrates on close examination because it lacks a proper human respect for the decay and death which are inherent in the passage of time. There may be something salutary and morally bracing in this view of time as progress; I believe the idea is quite defensible that there is progress in time, measured in terms of human satisfaction and achievement; and yet as a definition of time pure and simple it comes woefully short of the truth. What is later is not necessarily better than what is earlier, although it may be so; neither is it necessarily worse, of course; but the point is that time as such is not identical with progress in the human skills and arts and graces.

A second mistaken notion is that which identifies time with something called process. This neutral, colorless word may seem at first to be harmless enough, but that is just its danger. Its apparent neutrality covers, all too frequently, what is only a determination to have the last word to say on the subject of time. It acquires a certain prestige because it has been lifted out of the vocabulary of science; but one cannot avoid thinking that its users are more interested in reducing time, in factoring it out, than in recognizing it for what it is.

This second error is especially noticeable in modern naturalism. Starting with the commendable aim of "taking time seriously" and rightly concerned to avoid all "block-universe" theories of reality, naturalistic philosophers have put a premium on the category of dynamic change. Discovering that the world revealed through scientific methods could no longer be grasped by the old principle of substance, they made process a kind of philosophical watchword and in some instances did not hesitate to equate it with reality itself.

But what has happened to time within this modern mode of thought? By and large, it was simply dehumanized into process as before it had been superhumanized into progress. Naturalism offers process as the basic category of explanation which, it is supposed, goes deeper into what is real than time itself does. Ordinarily, naturalists speak of the "time-process," which suggests that time is one sort of process among others. In any case process seems in this view to be the more fundamental term. Especially in recent naturalism time tends to drop out of the picture in favor of process, and this is put forward as a better word for time than time itself.

Perhaps it is chiefly a matter of knowing what sort of time you are talking about, and in what perspective. But humanly lived time is not amenable to naturalistic reduction, not even when process is filled out with warmer terms such as novelty, creativity, or growth. Process under naturalistic auspices must always mean something less than the time we feel and know and have to deal with. This whole approach makes one suspect that humanly known time has gotten lost somehow in the analytical shuffle so that what remains is a curious pantemporalism from which time itself has been eliminated. Would there not be more reason in extending the notion of time to cover process, instead of this leveling down of time to process? What naturalism does, rather, is to drain the human content out of time and then diffuse it verbally throughout the universe in an unrecognizable form.

But we must not allow time to do a disappearing act in anyone's philosophy. Our human sense of time must be trusted, at least to give the data which rational thought must seek to interpret. It is significant, I believe, that we have to measure even vast periods of geological or astronomical change in terms of human time, which is the only time we can possibly know. At first glance there may not seem to be much in common between the "five minutes' walk" of the Boston guidebook and the "light-year" of the astronomer; but there is time in common, time as a dimension of human existence, which cannot be expelled from the most rarefied scientific observations.

And it must also be said that when time is permitted to drop out of process, as in naturalism, nothing much is left in the idea of process either. For process, if it means anything, means procession, that is, before-and-afterness, something that succeeds itself by superseding itself. In short, it means exactly what we know as time. This cannot logically be waived in favor of sheer flux, a pseudometaphysical ado and bustle; for then one merely explains away what has to be explained. Time is greater than process because it gives to process the only rational meaning it can have. Perhaps naturalism has not yet begun to take time seriously enough.

All this is bound to become clearer as we turn now to consider the present as the providential mode of time. I believe that it can be shown that the present has a distinctly Christian significance, arising from the conviction that in it man's time opens out upon God's time and bears upon its face the stamp of God's way with us. That conviction, as we shall see, is intimately linked with the doctrine that our destiny on earth is of real concern to him whose creatures we are and whom also we are meant to serve.

III

Students of the Bible have discovered in its pages an understanding of time which puts great emphasis upon the present moment as revealing God's intention for our life. Men as far apart in tradition and viewpoint as Nicolas Berdyaev, Oscar Cullmann, and John Marsh, to mention only a few, have made telling contributions to this end. Berdyaev's work is valuable in its delineation of the various contexts within which time has reality for us—the cosmic, symbolized by the circle; the historical, indicated by the line; and the existential, illustrated by the point. This last mode of time Berdyaev identifies as peculiarly biblical and Christian, but his insistence upon other modes keeps him from oversimplification and exclusiveness. Cullmann, on the other hand, has been eager to defend what is distinctively Christian and biblical in the conception of time against rival secular interpretations, both old and new. His real achievement is the relating of all events to the Christ-event of faith.

Marsh's book marks a genuine advance in this discussion. The author shares with Cullmann a profound fidelity to biblical perspectives but also resembles Berdyaev in wishing to illuminate by their help many pressing issues of human history and destiny in a much wider context. For Marsh is more than a biblical expositor who singles out key words and concepts given in Scripture in order to present a unified but narrow view of time; in the true sense he is a biblical philosopher who builds on scriptural foundations a responsible and far-ranging approach to the meaning of man's life.

"It is typical of Scripture," he writes, "not to locate an event by defining its place on a chronological scale, but to identify it by its content." [4] Not, of course, that the Bible is unacquainted with time-in-general as passage or transition; but even this awareness is held within a still stronger emphasis upon what Marsh calls realistic, or humanly lived, time—time, that is, as affording an opportunity to which we are to respond with some appropriate action. Thus there are times of natural events, social occasions, religious services, personal decision; and when any of these times have come, men are to seize the opportunity so presented by doing what is called for, what the time itself requires.

The same sort of thing has been said by others with equal force, but Marsh employs the biblical motif of opportunity-and-response not in order to distinguish the Christian faith so much as to relate its insights to the most common human experiences. So he finds in various biblical words for time some pertinent truths concerning

[4] *The Fulness of Time* (New York: Harper & Bros., 1952), pp. 20-21.

God at work in both nature and history. He takes considerable pains, in fact, to show that on the biblical view any sharp distinction between natural and historical happenings becomes highly dubious. In the Bible history and nature are both time-bound and together constitute the locale of our sin and our salvation wherein the opportunities that come to us are given by God. "Even in a simple thing like going to bed at night," says Marsh, "or rising at the beginning of the day; in sheltering from the rain, or gathering the harvest of the fields, man is really making response to the activity of God in time." [5] This remains true whether or not men respond rightly to the opportunities presented; it means what Marsh calls throughout his book the "theological transcendence of the chronological."

This view is general but also very specific. It holds together in an admirable way the universal and individual aspects of time. What is implied here is much more than some ultimate referring of daily life to the agency of God in a remote and distant sense; the point is that even commonplace things which we are prone to take for granted make possible the turning of man to God in believing and obedient love. Each and every time in which we have to live is offered by God and utilized by man; this is its very form and content. The faithful reader of the Bible is not provided automatically with a kind of measuring device for taking, as it were, the temperature of events; but he is placed within a temporal context of engagement with God, of entering into those events which are ordered by God for our good and for his glory. The question which a Christian believer asks about the time presented to him is rather like that of the small boy when he heard the circus was coming to town: "Do I get to be in it?" And his affirmative answer is made through the conviction that ordinary happenings are not mere happenstance but

[5] *Ibid.*, p. 22.

represent and body forth God's holy, mighty action upon and within time. Plainly, this begins to look a great deal like Providence, and in this direction we shall pursue the matter further.

Summing up, the biblical view of time embraces both passage, or *chronos,* and opportunity, or *kairos,* but with the accent falling characteristically on *kairos* as the fulfilling of *chronos.* We all must face the sobering fact that we live from that which is no more toward what is not yet through a slender, fragile boundary line called "now." Yet this is not the same as saying there is no permanence, no purchase on the real, in every passing moment as it comes along. To be sure, the moment as it presents itself is no more and no less than a point in time, before it has become past and after it is only future. But this same moment is also a viewpoint, a standpoint, and a point of departure. That is its original and *given* character which no philosophy of flux can ever quite think out of existence because the ceaseless shuffle of temporal passage never quite extinguishes it.

Let us say, then, that any present, my present, is no mere ripple in the stream of time as it rushes by, but instead a kind of rudder by which the stream becomes maneuverable and navigable, under God, by man's free choice and act. Of course each present moment merges imperceptibly into the next, and that into yet another; but this only means that there are fresh beginnings, second chances, all along the way. This wave of the present coming in on the vast tide of time—may it not in fact be the wave of God's right hand, allowing, assisting, and approving human endeavor? On these terms it is not impossible to believe that time itself witnesses not merely to the patience but also to the incredible forgiveness of God; indeed it becomes impossible not to believe so.

Yes, the present is man's time for freedom, man's God-given opportunity. Temporal successiveness has this remarkable way of shaping itself into temporal intensiveness, not of course invariably for my profit or my pleasure but wondrously for my good. The same truth is brought home by the familiar words of the ninetieth psalm, to which I have already referred: "So teach us to number our days, that we may apply our hearts unto wisdom." Usually, when we say that our days are numbered, we speak fatalistically; but in this text the rule appears to be, one thing at a time, no crying over spilled milk, let the morrow take care of itself. Our span of life, however brief or frail, is lined out and broken down into livable, workable portions—years, months, weeks, days, hours, minutes, seconds. Perhaps clocks and calendars do have something to tell us about Providence, after all. They mean that time is not entirely drift and waste. They remind us that the field of effort is always here, not somewhere else, and that the instant for decisive action is forever now, not then. That every day has its own number implies that it exerts its own claim and demands its own due. Is there not something truly providential about this experienced fact? It is highly significant that the form in which time comes to us is congruous with our mortal condition and is also adapted to our finite circumstances.

If we could once grasp the importance of the word "now," we Christians would know all we need to know, if not all we want to know, about the nature of time. The "now" is the "time being" which constitutes our only living clue to time past and time future, as it binds them both together. There has been a strong tendency in modern secular philosophy to regard the present as a "specious present," less real than the temporal flow within which it is cast up. According to this view the present seems more unique and decisive than it actually is, given the prior and conditioning fact of time-in-general. The more one stresses "real duration" as the nature of time, the less he values the present as time-in-particular. In this vein one may ask disparagingly how long the present lasts. A student once put this question to A. N. Whitehead, who answered mischievously, "About a tenth of a second, I think."

But a very different interpretation of the matter arises within the Christian perspective. There the present moment is not appearance merely but reality; it signifies quite precisely what time is all about. Every moment launched, rocketlike, into being is a providential present; it is actually presented to us as an opportune occasion claiming our response. Related first to God, from whom it comes to us, it bridges and embraces both past and future. Its reality is not extensive but intensive, not repeatable and general but specific and particular. And this, we believe, belongs to the character of time itself as the creature of God's sovereign concern.

In thinking thus about the providential quality of the present, we must again keep clear of certain errors into which our minds may easily fall. One is the existentialist notion that the present moment temporarily suspends or sets aside the flow of time by inserting nothing less than eternity into it. So T. S. Eliot writes, "History is a succession of timeless moments." Could anything be more unhistorical, indeed more antihistorical, than such a view? If God conditions time vertically rather than horizontally, to speak in spatial terms, by entering it by means of what Kierkegaard called "the Moment," then the significance of humanly lived time in both its duration and intensity soon disappears. We do the present no real honor and give God no true glory by this abstract collapsing of time into an artificial capsule of timelessness. The full import of this criticism will grow upon us as we begin to think of history and eternity in the following chapter. Here let us only observe that the present is providential for the very reason that it is presented to us horizontally and vertically at once (if we must use these spatial metaphors), that is, as a creative opening in time which engages our response. Thus *kairos* neither simply defies *chronos* nor merely duplicates it, but enables us to lay hold on time and move with God in time toward the fulfillment he intends for time.

Obviously the present is not all of time; but it is all the time there *is,* the only time that actually matters. The present consists of my response to opportunity in which my entire heritage is revalued and my whole destiny is prefigured. Hence we rightly extend the notion of the present beyond the "tenth of a second" mentioned by Whitehead; we speak of the present year, the present generation, or the present century. And this is as it should be, for the present is far more than an insertion into the flow of time; it is in fact a genuine link which bridges past and future and so qualifies both. In other words, time-in-particular belongs to the very nature of time-in-general. It tells us something true about God's purpose for time as a whole. It makes time what we know it to be.

Putting the matter in this light, we may correct some erroneous ways of thinking of both past and future to which our minds are prone. For example, we often tend to suppose that the past is no more than a scrap heap of dead, burned-out presents, rather like a pile of old spark plugs in a garage corner. Against this crude notion there are several points to be kept in mind. One is the power of memory, which is participation in the living past (see Augustine's masterly analysis in his *Confessions,* Book X, sections 8 through 25), not reproduction at a distance. Another is the fact that we usually do not recognize the hand of Providence at the moment when it actually structures time but only afterward as we "look back" upon that moment. How many people have found in some impairment of their faculties through cruel accident a veritable blessing and have made of it a blessing to others? The closing of one door of opportunity has often proved to be the opening of other even better doors. This must mean that the past is very much alive within the present, that it is not simply over and done with but retains something of its providential force. And thirdly, we must not neglect the fact that the past is the realm of discarded possibilities and missed opportunities; it is by no means only an accumulation of frozen bygone actualities. Thus guilt may be as much because of what was not done as because of what was done. One may even, as Robert Frost has observed, have hope for the past, namely, hope that the past will turn out to have been what it ought to have been. All these considerations look in the direction of an understanding of the past which sees it not as the antithesis or destruction of the present but as the preparation for and the extension backward of the present.

Are we not also likely to think of the future in equally irrelevant fashion? Thus we speak quite carelessly as if it were an "open book" consisting of blank pages on which human decision and action will some day write. But we have noticed already, in noting freedom, how the future, though of course uncertain, is not totally unknown or indeterminate. It consists in rather large measure of what Whitehead called "forms of definiteness," that is, concrete lures and goals. Our habit of attributing sheer potency to the future also overlooks another signal fact, namely, the character of human hope, which envisages the future as a coming present in which we live already in a spirit of "anticipated attainment."

In all this we are not discounting the real difference between past and future, but are insisting that it is not the difference between what is actual and what is possible. There is as much possiblity in the past as there is actually in the future, which is saying a great deal about both. Hence the proper key for understanding past and future, whether possible or actual, is exactly that of opportunity-and-response which also defines the providential present. And there it nothing fanciful or arbitrary in such a thought. It does not rid the world of its *chronos,* or before-and-afterness, but helps us to realize that it is *kairos,* or *nowness,* that determines the human significance of *chronos,* both fore and aft.

Paul Minear, writing from the viewpoint of biblical theology, discriminates between past and future as two kinds of movement in time, passingness and comingness. If we follow him in making this distinction, as I believe we should, we make it in the perspective afforded by what is being called the providential present. The present, as we know and live it, means that God himself is engaged in our existence and has a stake in it. It means that he will not and has not yet abandoned us. Both past and future merge in every present, and each present binds the past and future. These words from Martin Buber, the contemporary Jewish philosopher, put the case for a providential interpretation of the present strongly: "The present is not fugitive and transient, but continually present and enduring. ... The present arises only in virtue of the fact that the Thou (God) becomes present." [6]

God, then, so orders time that we are given a Now on which to stand and work and hope amidst its restless movement. This amounts to saying that even as we are creatures of time, so time is a creature of God. And that is saying a great deal indeed.

IV

One major conviction voiced by the doctrine of Providence is that God wills and works to maintain his creation at the same key or pitch of purpose for which he conceived and fashioned it. Theologians call this the preservation or conservation of the world. In the concluding portion of this chapter let us see how it bears upon our Christian understanding of time. Earlier I said in passing that conservation in the natural order corresponds with concurrence or cooperation in the context of human freedom. And these are distinctly interrelated levels of existence under God, which throw considerable light one upon the other.

If we believe that God conserves what he creates, we also believe that time is real to God as it is real to us. The very word "conservation" means, of course, continuance in being, identity in existence enduring through a span of time. Yet conservation also implies, and quite as clearly, that what is thus kept in being is

[6] *I and Thou* (New York: Chas. Scribner's Sons, 1937), pp. 12, 13.

somehow threatened by nonbeing. No created being is a necessary being. That is, it does not have to be just what it is, but could be something different. And it is not enough for a created being simply to be; it must he held in being if it is not to lapse into nothingness. Only what has been created can be conserved; but if it were not conserved, it would not be that which it was created to be. Here the reality of time, for both the creature and the Creator, is acknowledged.

Similarly, the very conception of Providence itself, of which conservation is an aspect, assumes that time is real for God. To provide means basically to see and plan ahead, and such foresight as our faith ascribes to God depends upon our human need to distinguish between present and future. For if God is able to look ahead, there must be some need for him to do so, taking thought or making provision for the future of that which is now present.

But even more important is the fact that the doctrine of creation itself includes the same emphasis upon the reality of time for God. The world of creatures, including man, is clearly not self-producing and self-explaining; that, indeed, is why the Christian name for nature is creation. Yet neither does our world merely refer back to God, as an effect implies a cause; it does not come ready-made from God as furniture or automobiles from a factory. No, it is constantly in the making, being made and remade, becoming what it is and being what it is meant to become. Time, therefore, is—if one may say so—of the essence of existence; it belongs to the very character of God's creative act. To say creation is to say that the world is not self-starting but has a beginning in God's purposeful action; it is to say that God creates the world in and with time. "The temporal," writes Emil Brunner, "is the essence of that which is created; as creatures we are temporal, all is temporal." [7]

[7] *The Christian Doctrine of Creation and Redemption* (Philadelphia: Westminster Press, 1952), p. 15.

As time is given with the creation, so it is also given throughout creation. It is more than God's way of acting on the world; it is his way of reacting to the world. Thus the Bible, for example, speaks frequently of God's patience, steadfastness, and even "repenting," all of which assume that our time is real for God. His way with us is not all suddenness and surprise, but also a standing by, a constancy, and an enduring. How shall we make this assumption clearer? One answer is that Providence means the successive re-creation of all God's creatures, which seems to be borne out by the continuous and temporal nature of creation itself. The fact that I am kept in being might mean that God creates me all over again, moment by moment. This would make Providence a perpetual miracle or tightly meshed chain of miracles; and time would not so much be laid down as the condition of our creaturehood as released or played out everlastingly and yet momentarily from God's hand.

There are, however, some real difficulties in this view. It is not because God adds another instant to my existence that my existence is prolonged by that instant. Neither faith nor reason requires us to believe this. I am preserved as God's creature because all my moments are cherished and embraced by the same God whose mighty act has launched time into being. God is characteristically creative and so is creative in each moment of time, giving, as Tillich says, "the power of being to everything that has being out of the creative ground of the divine life." [8] Tillich calls this God's "sustaining creativity." The point is that some measure of real time as opportunity-in-passage is required if such creative continuity is God's way of dealing with his creatures. By bending into time God does not pulverize or supernaturalize it; rather, he accepts it, moves with it, and redeems it. Thus my preservation is due to the fact that every

[8] *Systematic Theology*, I, 264.

moment is endowed with a sure sign of God's lordship over time in such a way that his own originating power becomes my sustaining power, structured into the very fiber of humanly lived time as its momentum and motive.

In other words, Providence as preservation means not the fragmentation or abrogation of time but instead the utilization and realization of time. From the fact that time is time and God is God, it does not follow that never the twain shall meet. If God cannot be said to disclose his will through and for time, he is clearly not the Lord in whose hands our times are held, as the thirty-first psalm puts it. And it even becomes questionable whether time can be said to be time, in the sense in which we have been thinking of it. Certainly it is not *kairos,* for that implies instrumentality and purpose in time; it may not even be *chronos,* if by this we mean real duration and successiveness.

On the whole, the relationship of man the creature to God the Creator via time was better grasped, I believe, by ancient and medieval thinkers than by modern ones, in spite of our fascinated preoccupation with the "problem" of time. To take but one illustration, Bonaventura thought that every creature on one side of itself tended downward toward destruction, while on the other side it strove to keep on being that which God intended. Like Albert the Great, he spoke of a bent toward nothingness, a kind of subterranean death wish, which is counterbalanced in the creature by a tendency toward union with the Creator. This older view, it may be noted with some astonishment, has strong affinities with both psychoanalysis and existentialist philosophy today.

The second and positive pole or tendency in creaturely life means our appropriate response, our providential *élan vital* or aptitude for seizing the opportunity which God presents to us in time. It is our way of moving through time with faith, hope, and love. Time is the context of estrangement from God; it is also the context of reconciliation with God. Placed as we are somewhere "east of Eden" on this side of man's fall into sinful, broken existence, perhaps it is our memory, however dim, of an original harmony with God which puts the engines of existence into reverse. The myth of Paradise, found in all ages and races, bespeaks this longing and moving back of the creature upon itself toward God.

What I have been expressing in theological prose may be better indicated by the metaphors of poetry. As Robert Frost has profoundly said, this movement of the human creature is

> Not just a swerving, but a throwing back,
> As if regret were in it and were sacred.

And his poem continues:

> Our life runs down in sending up the clock.
> The brook runs down in sending up our life.
> The sun runs down in sending up the brook.
> And there is something sending up the sun.
> It is this backward motion toward the source,
> Against the stream, that most we see ourselves in,
> The tribute of the current to the source.
> It is from this in nature we are from.
> It is most us.[9]

Is God's time our own time? No, for he is eternal. But our time is God's time; and this, as in Bach's great cantata, is the best of all times. Now we begin to see what it means to believe that our times are in his hand, that he who has been our dwelling place in all generations is our God from everlasting to everlasting.

Every passing present is a sign and wonder from God to us. It

- From "West-running Brook" by Robert Frost. Copyright, 1928, by Henry Holt and Company, Inc. By permission of the publishers.

is the pledge of his abiding presence, since it is called into being by his creative power, kept in motion by his patient providence, and is to be fulfilled according to his gracious promise. This is the veritable heart of time; it has not stopped beating ever since the morning stars sang together, and will not cease until God calls it a day. Through faith in him who abides yesterday, today, and forever we may hear it beating still.

5

From Everlasting to Everlasting

"'I am the Alpha and the Omega,' says the Lord God,
who is and who was and who is to come, the Almighty."
—*Rev. 1:8*

In a pregnant simile Reinhold Niebuhr suggests that human freedom is the warp while time is the woof of history, so that it is freedom which makes history into something more than what he terms natural time or process.[1] Although we have already challenged this reduction of the meaning of time, preferring to think of it as having its own dimension of freedom or opportunity, we can certainly agree with Niebuhr that time and freedom are actually woven together in the fabric of historical experience. By following up this clue of Niebuhr's we shall perhaps be able to complete the thought of the two preceding chapters and also come to grips with some of the issues involved in the interpretation of history from a Christian standpoint.

A great deal of our current interest in the meaning of history is really an impassioned concern with the question of destiny. Neither technical historiography nor any form of rational synthesizing can give a basic, satisfying answer. The question itself has to do with our history, to which we belong and contribute; it is a search for the story told by history, a story about everyman and the powers that be which either frustrate or fulfill his destiny. And this concern

---

[1] *Faith and History* (New York: Chas. Scribner's Sons, 1949), pp. 35, 37.

with history brings clearly into view the vast horizon of eternity, for one cannot think his way to the limits of historic time without also trying to think beyond them, asking why and how these limits are set and whether they may not in some degree be transcended. Of history and eternity, then, I shall make bold to speak within the present chapter.

I

First, let us tie in the idea of time we have been developing with the Christian way of understanding history. There is a good starting point in another remark of Niebuhr's—that "time is both the stage and the stuff of history." [2] To call time the stage of history means that it is a kind of metrical framework within which all historic actions transpire. It is time as passage and opportunity that takes the measure of historic changes so that they may be distinguished from and compared with one another according to some standard frame of reference. The very notion of the past which underlies any serious, systematic definition of history—whether as *res gestae,* things done, or *res scriptae,* things written down—at once introduces the age-old mystery of time in all its poignancy and force.

Yet time is not only a gigantic chronometer that ticks off all historic happenings; it is also their very substance or essence. More than a mere measuring rod applied to the mutations of history, time is mutability itself. More than the clocking of transitions, it is the stuff of transiency that winds up and runs down every clock. Time is indeed the measure of history but in the sense that it is both measuring and measurable. Let us call it, then, the raw material of all historic changes, the content as well as the bare form of such events. Thus history is to be understood not simply by reference to time but also as due to time, occurring by means of time. History

[2] *Ibid.,* p. 35.

takes place against the backdrop and beneath the curtain of time but also in time, with time, under the duress of time.

The second role of time in history is deeper than the first, since it alone gives meaning to the first. Only if time is the real continuum of history, can it provide the proper way of measuring history. That is, time is a stage which does a great deal more than simply mark the boundaries of history by giving breadth and depth and height to all eventful actions; time must somehow prod and push history itself into being. So time gives direction—the character of a one-way street—to history, quite as much as mere dimension. It constitutes the basis as well as the background of everything historical. We cannot therefore see time as the stage of history without recognizing it, too, as the very stuff of history.

A number of twentieth-century philosophers have attempted to do just this. Men such as Samuel Alexander, Whitehead, Heidegger, and above all Bergson have been describing time as the very flow or movement of reality itself, including history. They have held that time asserts itself with such inescapable force in human experience precisely because it exerts its own characteristic pressure in the nature of things. Unfortunately, this effort has not yet been treated by Christian theologians with the respect it deserves. This is probably because it has proceeded in large part upon frankly naturalistic assumptions which, as we have already seen, cannot satisfy the Christian mind. May one not, however, grant the truth, so far as it goes, even in a view of time that does not fully convince him? To say that time cannot be analyzed reductively into natural process does not mean, certainly, that time may not include and therefore express the true character of process. The only genuine alternative to naturalistic reduction is theological inclusion. Hence it is unfortunate that this new understanding of time should be dismissed rather than welcomed in Christian circles.

Often theologians go still further, accusing modern philosophers of idolizing time, deifying it, and so equating history or evolution on one hand with redemption or salvation on the other. Such an identification is undoubtedly erroneous, but this does not excuse us from conversing seriously with those who make it. By what right, it may be asked, does Niebuhr treat Bergson so cavalierly? In his eyes Bergson is a thoroughly secular thinker who tries to substitute time for God as the clue to ultimate meaning. His conception of *durée réelle,* thinks Niebuhr, is simply one more modern error to be exposed and removed. Granted that Bergson writes exuberantly about real duration and the *élan vital* as if he were apostrophizing time as the philosopher's absolute, but his so-called mystical attitude toward time is neither feigned nor contrived and may surely be otherwise interpreted than as a wish to deify it. When, for example, he portrays a "second type of knowledge," intuition, through which we are transported "by an effort of sympathy into the inwardness of becoming," [3] Bergson does not shut the door upon final mystery so much as open the door to it. If a thinker such as Bergson, or for that matter Heidegger, is led through contemplating time to adopt attitudes of lyrical eloquence and even reverence that set at naught his accustomed standards of rational coherence and factual adequacy, he can scarcely be blamed for trying to reduce history and nature to terms of simple intelligibility. Usually when philosophers write thus, it is because they are sharply conscious of the limitations of their thought, not because they are proudly bent on containing all mystery within the tidy garden of man's reason.

Or consider, if you will, the philosophy of Alfred North Whitehead as it deals with the matter of time. Like Bergson, he has spoken of a "creative advance" underlying the various time series, although his idea of epochs maintains a note of radical con-

---

[3] *Creative Evolution* (New York: Modern Library, Inc., 1944), p. 342.

tingency that is admittedly lacking in Bergson's thought. Moreover Whitehead's view that time is a "perpetual perishing" can hardly justify the theological criticism that here we have a typical modern confidence in progress, as Whitehead sees clearly the connection between time and death which Christian thought has always stressed. Nor is it right to charge such a philosophy with "secularism," since it understands the ancient contrast between change and permanence by means of the following view of God: "God and the World stand over against each other, expressing the final metaphysical truth. . . . In God's nature, permanence is primordial and flux is derivative from the World: in the World's nature, flux is primordial and permanence is derivative from God." [4] This view, it should be plain to any unprejudiced person, leads directly into a Christian interpretation of history and not away from it.

At bottom what keeps Christian theologians from granting a generous hearing to these accounts of time is their own preoccupation with a special philosophy of their own which has been temporarily baptized for the purpose of elucidating faith. This is the existentialist view which concentrates on what Kierkegaard called "the Moment"—the unique and isolated present which is thought not to be a given part of time at all but an insertion into it. Sometimes, indeed, this meaning of the temporal is regarded as superimposed upon the natural and historical meanings, which serve only as the setting for the break-through of the existential moment. According to this view real time is qualitative not quantitative, contemporaneous not continuous, subjective not objective. Thus the time of memory and hope, and that of passage therefore, are only a sort of drab and neutral background, indeed an empty stage for heightening and intensifying the significance of that time in which man freely makes his crucial decision for or against God.

[4] *Process and Reality* (New York: The Macmillan Co., 1929), p. 529.

This is markedly different from the thought developed in the last chapter that the Now of faith is an opportunity presented within and by time itself which belongs to its own nature as the work of God's creating and conserving purpose. This whole notion of the Moment remains a technical abstraction which ignores the fact that the necessity of choosing and acting in any present is something given by time itself. It represents a well-intentioned but really self-defeating effort to give Christian content to the "specious present" or tenth-of-a-second so worked over by modern philosophy and psychology. It cannot see that each and every moment of opportunity is made of the stuff of linear successiveness or passage. For one can hardly build up genuine history out of moments that are themselves timeless; that would add up to precisely zero so far as the historical is concerned. And therefore no moment, capitalized by faith or not, can be exempt from that coming-to-be and falling-away which constitutes the very meaning of the temporal and historical order.

This is why it will not do for Christian interpreters of history to contrive antinomies between *chronos* and *kairos* as if each did not get its meaning from the other. As Karl Löwith rightly says: "A historical now is not an indifferent instant but a *kairos*, which opens the horizon for past as well as for future. The significant now of the *kairos* qualifies the retrospect on the past and the prospect upon the future, uniting the past as preparation with the future as consummation." [5] This is but philosophical longhand for the fact already emphasized that every now is genuinely new. The same time-binding role of faith's decisive now has been ably set forth by Oscar Cullmann, who wishes to correct the excessive subjectivity of Kierkegaard.

If theology needs to stress real duration in order to conteract

[5] *Meaning in History* (University of Chicago Press, 1949), pp. 185-86.

the vogue of existentialism, secular philosophies also need the Christian insight that time affords real opportunity for man's freedom. This "extraordinary hovering between persistence and annihilation," as Emil Brunner calls man's implication in time, this raising of the questions "whence" and "whither" within our own awareness of time, opens out upon a still more central issue—that of time in relation to eternity.

II

God is eternal, man is temporal; but is that all we Christians have to say on this subject? Clearly not, for this is just where the deepest questions begin. We have to ask what each of these statements mean and what both mean together. Such a course is not optional but required if we are going to preach, pray, sing hymns, or read the Scriptures with understanding, much less give any sort of reason for our faith to those in our time who think time a treadmill and eternity a fiction.

Not a few philosophers and theologians have sought to state the issue in terms of the connection between time and the timeless. Reinhold Niebuhr seems to be among them, since he writes that the "question about time is how change is related to the changeless." [6] To put the matter thus, however, is to give a negative connotation to eternity which is quite foreign to Christian believing and living. We shall surely not understand the eternal only by means of what it lacks. It is better to find common ground with those who conceive eternity as being and time as becoming, for whom eternity is the principle of life and positive power, operating within and upon time itself.

Without wishing in the slightest to deny that there is a real question about how change is related to the changeless, one must

6 Op. cit., p. 36.

still point out that it is not exactly the question about time and eternity. To put it so suggests that one is opposing the mobile to the rigid, the dynamic to the static, on the dogmatic assumption that eternity is a condition of fixity or rest while time is a sort of perpetual-motion machine. But this only oversimplifies a most intricate and profound issue. There are rigidities in time, very like what astronomers call "prominences" on the sun's surface—regularities, aggregations, culminations, repetitions, yes, the past itself—and there is something in eternity suggesting vitality or energy, or else we Christians would not keep on associating the word with life and God. One might even make out a good case for saying that necessity, law, and limitation belong to time and not eternity while spontaneity and dynamism are inherent in eternity and not time, or at any rate in the working of eternity in time.

Among the many interpretations of the time-eternity relationship that have borne fruit in Christian thought, surely the greatest has been that of Plato. If only because of its deep and lasting influence it should be better understood. Of late it has been the fashion to accuse the Greeks, and Plato in particular, of employing the ideas of time and eternity to split the universe—theoretically and verbally, of course—in two. This charge, however, which fits so neatly into textbook patterns leaves the actual reader of Plato curiously cold. In what sense can it possibly apply to Plato's celebrated teaching that time is the "moving image of eternity"? That doctrine, as I firmly believe, stands against all attack as the most adequate statement in non-Christian thought of what the Christian faith understands to be true concerning their relation.

Plato's well-known phrase certainly expresses a contrast but also a profound connection. Eternity and time are not the same; neither is time a mere duplicate or copy of eternity. Whatever time may be, it is not a rubber stamp of anything else. And no image is identical with reality, obviously enough, even though it may serve as a reliable clue to the nature of the real; yet it is after all an image and as such a "life-symbol," to use Susan Stebbing's phrase, rather than a mere index or pointer. That is, an image can be trusted to suggest the real because it is vested with the character of that which it reflects and expresses. Plato dared to ask a question about the *being* of becoming and answered that it consisted in a sympathetic acting out or mimesis of the eternal.

As in Christian so in Platonic thought the question about time is fundamentally that about the world's relation to God. In this sense Whitehead, for example, is thoroughly within the Platonic tradition. For Plato, God is the originator of the eternal forms in which all temporal facts participate; he is the "Maker and Father of all things" who purposes to make the world "as like himself as possible." Time, then, for Plato as for Christianity is a creature of God, although naturally not in the biblical sense. Yet one is not at liberty to push the obvious differences too far. Plato teaches that time is something made by God which bears on its face the marks of likeness, nay, of dynamic kinship, to its Maker.

The view that time is the moving image of eternity has some important consequences. First, eternity is not merely timelessness or changelessness; for Plato it is never simply a logical contradiction to time. Thus he writes with impassioned eloquence in the dialogue called the *Sophist:* "Can we, O heavens, ever be made to believe that motion and life and soul and mind are not present in absolute Being? Can we imagine Being to be devoid of life and mind and to remain a venerable, holy, mindless, unmoving fixture?" In light of this and many similar passages it becomes little short of astounding to read in Brunner that Plato views eternity as timelessness.[7] Could even John Dewey, one wonders, have spoken more emphatically than Plato for the contrary view? When Plato speaks,

[7] *Eternal Hope* (Philadelphia: Westminster Press, 1954), pp. 47, 53, etc.

for example, of eternal truth, he does not mean that such truth exists somehow out of all relations to time or that it lacks the quality of temporality, but rather that truth itself possesses a character that makes it always *timely* with respect to any situation which can possibly occur.

A second consequence is that eternity is not the unending prolongation of time, a definition recently put forward by Cullman and Ferré among others. On this view eternity becomes only more time, never more than time. Platonic thought, however, just like classical Christian theology, always understands time by reference to eternity and not eternity solely by means of time. A truth, to use this example again, is not eternal by virtue of extensive applicability to innumerable facts; its relevance to them arises from the prior fact that they exemplify and body forth, in fragmentary yet essentially faithful ways, the eternal reality on which they depend for both being and being known. This is why for Plato every discovery of truth is a confirmation in experience of what is already known in eternity, as when the illiterate slave in the *Meno* proves the Pythagorean theorem under the skillful cross-examining of Socrates.

The removal of these two false meanings of eternity leaves only the third and true one standing—that eternity is the mode of being which includes time by transcending it. Once again, to use truth as the illustration, its eternal character consists precisely in being altogether reliable, available, and inexhaustible regardless of the various perspectives within which it is grasped or the diverse occasions which may prompt men to discover it. Eternal truth is truth "no matter what," which is to say that it is ever-timely, neither timeless nor overextended temporally. The same applies to anything that can with justice be called eternal.

Plato's view of eternity as the inclusive transcendence of time is, despite the protestations of Brunner and Niebuhr, very close formally to our Christian understanding of the same relationship, however far apart they may be in terms of content. At least it is as close to faith as non-Christian philosophies are likely to come. The great Augustine saw this and insisted upon it, which has earned him the astonishing reputation of a heretic among recent theological purists. Nevertheless he said a quite definitive Christian word upon this subject. To Augustine as to Plato, while eternity may and does become temporal, time cannot become eternal. Here one might say the relationship between eternity and time is analogical rather than merely paradoxical, although there is no suggestion that the terms are interchangeable. This view contains no self-imposed cleavage or obstacle such as Berdyaev has in mind when he declares: "The cleavage between the eternal and the temporal is both the greatest delusion of consciousness and an obstacle to the foundation of a true philosophy of history." [8] Since the true philosophy of history is plainly for Berdyaev the Christian one, his comment may not unfairly be applied to current efforts to accentuate and deepen the cleavage which he so deplored. Why should it be assumed without question that Christian faith posits an absolute disjunction between time and eternity? Does it not follow that only sheer miracle and utter paradox can account for the way in which eternity enters time and ransoms it through Jesus Christ? But surely a Christian must see history as the very crossroads of eternity and time, for he trusts profoundly in the God who works eternally to reconcile the temporal order to himself and hopes even against hope for the final triumph of God's eternal purpose over, yet also within, the passing opportunities which time offers men.

We mortals never step out of time into eternity, not even in the lonely instant when destiny is at stake and we decide for God. Time cannot be a synonym for eternity but remains at best a falter-

---

[8] *The Meaning of History*, p. 75. Used by permission of Geoffrey Bles Ltd.

ing and flickering symbol of the eternal. Furthermore, like all real symbols, time retains a certain stubborn nature of its own which keeps it from becoming more than an image of that which it so indubitably bodies forth. As time itself perpetually suggests by its incessant imitative movement more than it can possibly contain, so eternity reflects and gives itself as being within the broken mirror of temporal becoming.

This has been put so finely by Berdyaev that I can only quote his words:

The historical character of Christianity may be attributed to the fact that the Christian consciousness had conceived eternity as manifesting and incarnating itself in time. The significance of Christianity as it manifests itself in the temporal and historical process lies in its demonstration that eternity or the divine reality can break the chain of time, penetrate into and appear as the dominant force in it. It postulates not only history but also time, without which it cannot exist. And yet it represents a constant struggle between the eternal and the temporal, a constant resistance of eternity to time, a constant effort of the eternal principle to achieve a victory over time. But the victory it seeks implies neither a departure from time, nor a denial of it, nor again the adoption of a position detached from it. For this would imply the denial of history itself.[9]

This yields, I firmly believe, the only rationally adequate framework for interpreting in structured, sober fashion what the Christian faith teaches on the matter. Without real time there can be no real history; and apart from real history there is no real incarnation, revelation, or redemption. But what makes time real? Precisely that it is anchored in the being of eternal God. To adopt the spatial way of speaking which is evidently so much to the current taste, time

[9] *Ibid.*, pp. 67-68. Used by permission of Geoffrey Bles Ltd.

is related horizontally as well as vertically to eternity, which is of course only to say that it is related *temporally* to eternity.

The Christian Platonism here defended will not, obviously, go the whole way with Plato either in regarding cultural epochs as mythical stages in the cosmic drama or in equating the eternal too easily with the universe itself. The once-for-allness of the event of Jesus Christ forbids the placing of our full weight upon either history-myths or nature-cycles. Nothing is to be gained by supposing that Plato was a kind of Christian in disguise. He did not believe in the Incarnation, yet he provided us who do with the sort of philosophy in which the Incarnation makes sense. What is needed, clearly, is not simply a borrowed but a converted Platonism in which the eternal not only grounds the temporal but bends into it and responds to it as God in the full Christian meaning of that word. Yet this will not prevent us from agreeing with Plato on the view that time and eternity are so linked in reality that the temporal is important because the eternal is supreme.

Also a Christian will hesitate to follow Plato in thinking that the human soul is eternal and will be even more reluctant to call the universe eternal, as Plato does. We shall emphasize the note of struggle in the relationship of eternity to time, far more than Plato; but with him we shall believe that it is fundamentally the struggle between substance and shadow, reality and reflection, life and death —a struggle carried on even within time itself.

Once more, we know better than Plato that the things which are seen are temporal while the things that are not seen are eternal (II Cor. 4:18); but let us not forget that we learned it from Plato. To us, after all, faith itself is the evidence, or seeing, of things not seen (Heb. 11:1)—a sort of provisional paradox, if you like, which nevertheless asserts the glorious possibility that we time-bound mortals may glimpse

through all this fleshly dress
Bright shoots of everlastingnesse.

III

What then of the relationship between eternity and history? In working out an answer there are two guiding principles to be observed, as has already been indicated. The first is that time, the stage and stuff of history, is anchored in the depths of the eternal; the second, which will now require attention, is that the eternal comprehends and consummates the historical. No one has ever been more faithful to these principles than Augustine, who without abandoning the classical view that God is perfect activity beyond the destructive changes of temporal history, yet also affirmed the biblical conviction that history with all its changes is the working out of God's eternal vision and power.

Augustine does not brush aside impatiently the philosophical puzzles posed by the so-called problem of time, but treats them with sensitive regard and analytical competence. He does not, however, treat these matters in objective isolation from the promptings of his Christian faith. In his mind they assume the form of this question: What is the relation between man's time, history, and God's time, eternity? He gives his answer in terms of the principle of inclusive transcendence, as we shall shortly see.

Consider in this light the passage which comes near the beginning of the *Confessions:*

For You are infinite and in You there is no change, nor does today pass away in You. Yet in another sense in You it does pass away, for in You are all such things—they could not even have any being that could pass away unless You upheld them in being. And because Your years do not pass, Your years are today; and no matter how many our days and our fathers' days have been, they have all passed in Your undying day and from it have received such being and measures as they had; and all the days to come shall similarly pass in Your undying day and shall receive from it their being and measures. But You are still the same. All our tomorrows to the end of time You shall make to be in this Your day; and all our yesterdays from the beginning of time You have made to be in this Your day.[10]

For Christian thinking in the Platonic and Augustinian tradition the fundamental concern is to understand historical temporality in view of the eternal spontaneity of God in whom, as Augustine says earlier, infinite Being is identical with infinite Life. Far from representing treason to biblical faith, this concern is but the desire to explicate that faith in terms as nearly consonant as possible with itself. Emphatically it is not a matter of making purely rational adjustments between the notions of change and the changeless, nor of reconciling theoretically by means of the Thomist definition of "simultaneity" the opposing categories of duration and immediacy in God. It is only the constant concern of daily faith in Providence itself—that of grounding yesterday and tomorrow in the everlasting Now of God, and of discovering real historic meaning in the fact that God, who is above the shocks and changes of time, yet fashions and bends them according to his will. Yes, the contrast which both conditions and challenges our faith is not between the time-bound and the timeless; it is between the passing and the abiding, between a world that is never the same and God who is always the same. And this contrast, since it appears within the surge of temporal history itself, establishes—so we Christians believe—the major clue to its interpretation.

To revert, then, to the old wooden notion that eternity means static perfection or immobility would make anything like genuine Providence unthinkable. The same negative effect, moreover, comes

<hr>

[10] Bk. I, 6.

from conceiving eternity as endless time; for no reduplication of time, however overextended, can bring about that redemption of time which our faith sees God working to achieve. The true and Christian meaning of eternity is that suggested by the biblical statement that with the Lord God a thousand years is as one day (Ps. 90:4; II Pet. 3:8). We have some real hints of this meaning within our own experience of time; thus memory as Augustine describes it is not simply a looking back, but a living on of the past within the present, and hope is not mere expectation but a positive earnest of things to come. That this time-binding, time-bracketing possibility is open to man suggests to faith in strongest terms that it is actual in God. And so conceived, eternity takes on its Christian meaning of timeliness and timefulness.

What then shall be said of history? It is the place where God's abidingness meets and proves itself a match for man's successiveness. This contrast, to be sure, is felt and lived within the time span itself; but it is not a purely temporal contrast. What has already been argued regarding the relationship between passage and opportunity in time should make this clear. Neither can we follow Erich Frank, A. P. Shepherd, and others in assuming that eternity and time are ultimately one—unless this be interpreted eschatologically, not philosophically. Our faith affirms, on the contrary, that man's time is created, comprehended, and concluded in God's own good time. That is why we have to reject both the pantemporalism of modern naturalism and the exaggerated antitemporalism of Kierkegaard, who wrote in what must surely have been an unguarded moment that the "eternal . . . has absolutely no history." [11]

Opportunity is not superimposed upon passage, nor inserted into it, by God; it is the working of eternity in and through and on

[11] *Philosophical Fragments* (Princeton, N. J.: Princeton University Press, 1936), p. 62.

behalf of time, as the inner momentum of time. Since passage and opportunity make up together the texture of man's time, God's time must therefore be seen in faith as genuine everlastingness, a compound and not a simple term of thought. This may be put a bit differently by saying that eternity is as much God's response to time as his nontemporal priority over it. Hence it is eternity that makes our history truly *historic,* because it is God who conditions, continues, and completes our history. The story within history lies precisely here. God's undying day is likewise his everlasting Yea spoken to the strivings and struggles of historic humanity.

If only by planting the Cross at the crossroads of history, Christian faith declares that man's time opens out upon God's time and that God's time once for all enters man's time to save it from the threat of self-destruction. No one who looks at the death of Christ can fail to see there the central, crucial token of the fact that history has meaning and abiding worth within the eternal counsel of God. Neither can faith in the Cross ever believe that God's eternity makes no response to and leaves no room for man's own time-containing life. Rather it affirms: Jesus Christ, the same yesterday, today, and forever—thereby linking his saving work with the everlasting providence of God.

The Christian reading of history takes man's time with such complete seriousness because it takes God's time with even greater seriousness. Upon eternity depends our history for whatever being and measures it may have. Our past, present, and future are intended by and included within the everlasting day of God. Perhaps we can only express this indirectly and obliquely by saying that all time is present to God. For according to the teaching of our faith God does not remember or expect; he simply *knows.* He is aware of our past and our future, but not as his past and his future. Although our time is ultimately his, his time is not identical with ours.[12]

Our history like time itself is therefore real to God, but in a different way from that in which it is real to us. As it passes away, our temporal history does not disappear or drop out of God's sight, any more than it materializes out of nothing as it comes to be. It is from God and to God and in God, however much it may seem to transpire in spite of God. In passing it is taken up, readmitted into God's undying day, into the eternal Life from which it came. And it is treasured by God on account of what it has meant for us who have lived through it, so that it does not lose for him the character of passage and opportunity which it has for us.

Yes, the eternal does have a history, *pace* Kierkegaard. Not that eternity is somehow enveloped and tied down within history, but that history is created, cared for, and completed by eternity. A Christian Platonism, far from seeking to give history the last word, is par excellence an affirmation of the priority of the eternal. Together with a sharp and telling sense of the transiency of all temporal things, this way of viewing places equal if not greater stress upon eternal God, whose years shall have no end and who endures while generations and ages rise and fall away (Ps. 102:26-27). And when the emphasis is thus rightly placed, history may be truly said to have eternal significance—that is, significance in and for eternity. Because all human happenings are conditioned by God's creating power, subject to his constant judgment, upheld by his patient wisdom, and cherished in his redeeming purpose, they form together a living fabric of memory and hope, of decision and destiny, into which God has entered and with which he is mightily and everlastingly engaged.

May we not then speak of a celestial or saving as well as a terrestrial or chronological history, following the fathers of the

---

[12] For some of the finer points see the discussion between Tillich and Charles Hartshorne in *The Theology of Paul Tillich,* ed. C. W. Kegley and R. W. Bretall (New York: The Macmillan Co., 1952), pp. 173-74, 339-40.

church and especially Augustine? Yes, but only if we do not understand this distinction geometrically in terms of parallel or intersecting lines. Celestial history is not a fundamentally different thing from human history as we know and live it; it is rather that same history on its Godward side, raised to the highest power and so realizing God's intention for itself. Human history becomes saving history only because it is the history of the eternal—a movement or drama carried forward by God's will and so somehow transpiring within his very life.

In speaking thus we rid ourselves completely of the dogma of the inert, immobile Absolute which has too often been confused with the Lord God of Christian and biblical faith. We abandon it in favor of the doctrine that God works patiently, enduringly, to bring his eternal plan to fruition in historic time. I said "enduringly"; may not this commit us to the view that God has to endure, has perhaps even to suffer? It is impossible, as Berdyaev points out, "to assert the tragic destiny of the Son of God and His expiatory death without at the same time admitting movement in the divine life." [13] That much is clearly indicated, but what sort of movement in God do we mean to affirm? Those who speak of God as suffering in Christ have generally had in mind God's susceptibility or passivity. But there are many modes of suffering, not all of which are identical with pain or finitude. I should myself prefer to maintain that the passion of the Son is the disclosure of the compassion of the Father, and that therefore the Father suffers with rather than in the Son. What else could the Trinity possibly involve as a Christian doctrine? Our God moves through history without ceasing to be God. As Calvin liked to say, he was on earth without leaving heaven.

No fabricated theoretical parallelism or interactionism of eternity and time can express this conviction at all adequately. From the per-

[13] *The Meaning of History*, p. 48.

spective of time, which is the only one we mortals know, eternity appears as abidingness or everlastingness, with its personal aspects of patience, steadfastness, and trustworthiness of which the Bible speaks so fervently and often. In other words, only the doctrine of Providence can do justice to the Christian faith at this point, since it is Providence which signifies the timeful and the timely in God's way with man.

On these terms, too, the old conception of a divine humanity becomes again relevant. Startling as it is to those who have been underscoring the total otherness of God to everything human, this great patristic idea has undoubted roots in the New Testament. Put most simply, it is the truth that God became man in order that men might become Godlike themselves. At the very least this means, to quote Berdyaev once again, that "history is, indeed, not only the relevation of God, but also the reciprocal revelation of man in God." [14] Redemption, after all, is not solely a negative word signifying deliverance but a positive word signifying companionship and even communion. And this is what God is about in history, that we should know ourselves as what he intends us to be.

That history is redemptively and providentially related to eternity has been the major burden of this chapter. If God discloses himself anywhere in history at all, the whole of history must be his field of competent concern. This is why the writer of the Fourth Gospel has the Christ say, "Before Abraham was, I am" (8:58), and why Matthew attributes to him that other saying so treasured by Christian people, "Lo, I am with you always, even unto the end of the world" (28:20 A.S.V.). Not only does the eternal have a history, but history suggests within itself the very eternity by which it is sustained and structured.

If this is true regarding revelation, it is even truer of the re-

[14] *Ibid.,* p. 57.

sponse to relevation which is Christian faith. Existentialists may measure faith in terms of the Moment, but not the Bible. On the contrary, the Bible gives the distinct impression that the moment is a rather poor index of the authenticity of faith. Instead it describes faith in terms of enduring to the end, bearing and hoping all things, anchoring every present in the rock and refuge of God's everlastingness. Faith then is basically fidelity, our human way of answering to God's own steadfastness, our laying hold upon the sovereign and staying love that will not let us go.

Let us then sum up the thought of this chapter. Christian teaching about Providence in its bearing upon human destiny requires us to make three affirmations. First, time is real because history, in which remembered past is tied to anticipated future by way of genuine duration, is also real. Second, eternity is real because time, which witnesses profoundly to its own derived, fragmentary, and essentially imitative nature, is also real. And finally, history is real because eternity, which makes, includes, and saves it, is also real. So understood, there is no cleavage between the historical and the eternal except that which human sin itself has caused. But sin is deception as well as disobedience, and its view of the relationship between man's time and God's time can scarcely be taken as the true one. Rather, faith lives and works and looks ahead by virtue of the mighty persuasion, to which theology can give but halting and tremulous expression, that the Lord God is our Alpha and Omega, the Eternal, who is and was and is to come.

6

Of Faith and the Tragic

"If God be for us, who can be against us?"—*Rom. 8:31 (K.J.V.)*

No one would deny, I think, that life today is wearing a tragic mask for multitudes of people. This is not so much a piling up of personal misfortunes as it is a certain deep-seated mistrust, a stylized suspicion of life which embraces our behavior and shapes our beliefs. Thus once again the sinister and sullen thought is growing that existence is a sort of calamity or vicious circle within which men stand defenseless and alone. This thought is made persuasive, if scarcely attractive, by the recent course of world history. And even where it remains unspoken, it is nonetheless keenly felt and stubbornly recurrent, like a twinge of bodily pain which though unbidden comes as no stranger to us. The result is that tragedy is fast regaining its ancient place as a dominant form for interpreting our life in the world.

This reawakening of the tragic sense of life exerts a double sort of pressure upon those of us who are trying to maintain another outlook, deriving its source and standard from convictions that are frankly and robustly Christian. Not only does it challenge; it must counsel and correct us, insofar as we go on making too facile adjustments and too glib generalizations in the presence of the tragic. In short, the question we have to face is this: Can Christian faith reckon adequately and effectively with an interpretation of the meaning of our life in grimly tragic terms?

I

Of course the question about Christianity and tragedy may be taken in several different ways. It may refer quite superficially to the general tone or temper of Christian believing, inquiring only whether our faith is predominantly pessimistic or optimistic. Do we tend to take a dim view of human capabilities and eventualities or one that is encouraging, serene, and bracing? Are we on the whole a fearful or a hopeful lot? However interesting it might be to sketch a kind of profile of the Christian temperament, this way of putting the question is rather beside the point. It sidesteps every actual issue posed for faith by tragic happenings, through the shoddy device of affixing labels prematurely; and more dishonestly, it transposes what is surely an inquiry about ultimate reality into the far lesser one of psychological tonality.

Or secondly, the question may be asked as if it were simply a matter of discovering whether a logical choice must be made between the tragic and the Christian view of things, or whether on the other hand they can be intellectually harmonized. This would simply treat them as contrasting, potentially competitive philosophies; but it would soon come down to the deeper question whether tragic events are incidental and surmountable or rather intrinsic and inevitable. From here on out it would be easy to reduce this to the old unsolved puzzle regarding the place of evil in the world. Does it pertain to the substance or merely the shadow of things? Does it have for Christians an ultimate or only an intermediate, transitional importance? But if this is all we mean by the question, we are looking only for some articulate philosophical framework on which faith may be supported. We are not delineating faith itself, but merely justifying what we assume on other grounds to be true. An exclusive interest in rational and systematic clarity ignores all too often the very bite and pang of the question; it only bypasses its personal and existential force upon the questioner. Surely there is something mysterious in the tragic that cannot be absorbed without remainder into what is simply problematic.

There is, however, a third way of posing this question which commends itself more nearly and warmly to the serious-minded Christian. That is to ask it neither psychologically nor philosophically alone, but theologically, as having to do with God's relationship to human destiny. Does Christian faith, as it is lived and known, recognize the tragic character of destiny as something which discloses the true purpose of God? On further thought this question breaks down into two others, distinct in form though interwoven in fact. Does faith in God squarely face and competently reckon with whatever is tragic in existence? That is the first. How does our faith relate the tragic in both thought and life to God's intention and control? That is the second. And while this framing of the question naturally does not forbid concern with psychological attitudes or philosophical assumptions, it makes one point decidedly clear—that every question about the tragic is at bottom a question about God.

The impression has certainly gotten abroad that Christian thinking becomes quite inept and baffled whenever it has to confront tragedy. Some of the leading and most influential writers of our day do not hesitate to make this charge. Take, for example, Karl Jaspers, the philosopher of Basel, with whom we shall be carrying on a running conversation in this chapter. Although he is a university teacher, there is nothing academic in the issues he brings forward. On the contrary, they bear directly and poignantly upon every Christian's way of life. They have to do with how we take what happens to us and so cannot and must not be avoided.

Jaspers sets his own interpretation of the tragic in deliberate and sharp contrast with what he believes to be the Christian view. In fact he goes so far as to declare that "no genuinely Christian tragedy can exist . . . what is essential to the Christian cannot even emerge in tragedy . . . tragic knowledge must escape the Christian." [1] Why is this? Because, says Jaspers, Christianity regards tragic events as always pointing beyond themselves to something else, being either unwilling or unable to face the fact that they are basic to human existence. Speaking of the dramas of Racine and Calderón, for example, he claims that what is genuinely tragic in them is extinguished by the clear and confident light of Christian truth, which therefore suffuses and indeed supplants the tragic.

Thus although Jaspers grants that Christianity succeeds in establishing a "real polarity" between God on the one hand and the sinful, suffering human world on the other, he insists that its final emphasis is necessarily upon the transforming, overriding power of God. And naturally this gives God, not tragedy, the last word with man. Christian faith is through and through providential. Its vision of divine perfection and ultimate blessedness, he thinks, must invariably set at naught whatever threat or peril may be thrown in man's earthly way. So for faith in God each barrier becomes a hurdle, every stumbling block a stepping-stone, to victory, security, and peace. The immediate pang of sorrow is overcome by the ultimate assurance that God has power to heal and save everything that belongs to him. It therefore follows according to Jaspers that Christianity has no real tragic sense at all and, lacking it, no actual capacity for facing and assimilating the kind of human situation for which his own graphic word is "shipwreck."

Jaspers' verdict as to the essentially untragic character of Christian faith is something less than devastating, however. He rather definitely qualifies these uncompromisingly negative assertions. For example, he admits that the Christian effort to cope with what is

---

[1] *Tragedy Is Not Enough* (Boston: Beacon Press, 1952), pp. 38, 39. Used by permission of the publisher. This essay is a translated portion of Jasper's major work on truth (*Von der Wahrheit*).

tragic, if not to comprehend it, is "charged with a new kind of tension" unmatched elsewhere in the world's great faiths. He goes on to grant that by substituting Providence for pagan fate or destiny, Christianity generates a "unique kind of seriousness" in human history—and he does not seem to be referring merely to the Inquisition or the Crusades either. Again, he himself takes the view that man's deliverance from tragedy can come only through a "faith that knows another reality besides immanental reality," which suggests that his own interpretation approaches the Christian one at several critical points.[2]

Yet in spite of these more sympathetic comments Jaspers holds to his central verdict. So he insists that with Christian poets such as Dante a noteworthy transformation of the tragic has occurred. He writes:

> With them, knowledge of the tragic, the tragic predicaments themselves, and tragic heroism, have all undergone radical change because these poets have included them within the plan of Providence and the operation of Grace, a plan and an operation that deliver man from all the vast nothingness and self-destruction in this world.[3]

Jaspers believes then that Christianity removes the really tragic character of human existence by refusing to regard it as an authentic disclosure of the way things finally are. Because we Christians claim to know something else besides the tragic which transfigures it and brings deliverance from this transitional world of pain and guilt and death, we are unable to deal either realistically or relevantly with the tragic. That is Jaspers' charge. To him, in fact, Providence can only mean the unwarranted transformation of the tragic.

This poses our original question in a still more insistent form.

[2] *Ibid.*, pp. 30, 82.
[3] *Ibid.*, pp. 82-83.

Does Christian faith admit and make use of a tragic principle in what it teaches concerning man's being-in-the-world? Or is what I have been calling its providential principle the unjustified transformation of the tragic? Let us see if we can find an answer.

II

A good way to begin is by defining what we Christians do mean by tragedy and the tragic. Few words, one fears, are used so casually and loosely today. They are applied without discrimination to almost any melancholy state or distressing occurrence, as if they were but synonyms for whatever is pitiful or disappointing. This could be called, and not altogether unkindly, the toothache view of tragedy.

All this chronic vagueness has at least two unhappy consequences. One, obviously, is a growing liability to self-pity whenever I attach these words to my own misadventures, as if I were the innocent victim of life's bad jokes. The sense of being "put upon" increases with one's willingness to see the tragic almost everywhere he looks. So when I call some transient ailment or nagging annoyance the "cross" I have to bear, I may be relating my earthly pilgrimage and warfare in a positive manner to the suffering love of God in Jesus Christ; but on the other hand, I may be just a bit overeager to identify my way with the Lord's. It is not always easy to draw the line between maturity and morbidity in these matters, but the line is there.

The second effect is even more debilitating. As the tragic sense becomes more and more diffused, it is bound to lose its own specific gravity and point. Here as always, hypersensitiveness is the sworn enemy of a true sensibility; and an effective holding action waits upon some measure of healthy-minded discrimination. It is unfortunately the case that in proportion as almost any mischance may seem to be tragic, none is really so. This dissipation and dilution of the tragic might be called one of the more degrading features of our own time.

Shall we say then that we have no right to go on using such words as tragedy and the tragic? By no means, for there is a dimension of our life to which they do apply with sobering relevance. A young wife and mother widowed by an airplane crash, a preacher stricken with cancer of the throat, a little child crippled and bent by paralysis—these are undeniably tragic in anybody's language. The tragic is that plane of human existence where fulfillment is threatened by frustration and one's very being is menaced by nothingness. It is moreover an inclined plane on which this threat is somehow being made good and a losing battle has to be fought. Yes, tragic experience is always more than simple downfall, no matter how catastrophic; and more than mere deterioration, no matter how pathetic. It means reversal, turning of the tide against man, which can easily be understood as hostility of destiny toward man.

The tragic is no single type of happening such as loss of sight or hearing, for example, although these may very well signal its presence. It is an aspect touching each and every human experience insofar as it is imperiled and insecure—and what experience is not? —as when we say that the worst is the corruption of the best or that something carries in itself the seeds of its own destruction. Neither is the tragic a simple quality attached to experience which can be factored out and isolated, theoretically or practically, as if one did not really belong to it. An engagement with the tragic is what logicians call sometimes an "entailment," that is, an involvement of oneself in being and not being. It is at once an encounter and an estimate, event and meaning both together, and so betrays the character of what we have been calling mystery. One may say that the tragic is both a condition and a category of our destiny as it takes shape within and around us.

Notice that now I am speaking of the tragic, not of tragedy.

The difference is important. The tragic is an aspect of destiny itself, a kind of grave and mournful accompaniment to man's being-in-the-world. It is, as has already been said, not simply fact but the form in which facts appear to us. And as we attend more and more to the latter, the conception of tragedy comes into view. Tragedy is the formalized interpretation of the tragic, given in its own terms and on its own ground.

It is surely not accidental that the word "tragedy" should be commonly restricted to a particular type of dramatic literature. The dictionary definition, "the sort of dramatic action in which the outcome is grave, often catastrophic or fatal, for one or more of the characters involved," does not afford much theological help, since it makes tragedy a blanketing and not a probing term. Nevertheless such a definition may be useful in reminding us that tragedy is not alone a description but also an interpretation of what happens to human beings in this kind of world. It is, in short, a certain way of schematizing or stylizing our experience. So Aristotle in his famous definition called tragedy the "imitation of an action," that is, a masking and miming of human experience by which it is invested with a particular look or shape.

Thus where the tragic means the vulnerable and perishable nature of all our life, nothing more or less, tragedy goes far beyond this. For tragedy sees human adversity in its literal sense of over-againstness, which might better be called up-againstness. Job has his Adversary and Cap'n Ahab his White Whale. What we may term the tragedic conflict is always an unequal one; the human being caught up in it is finally overwhelmed and brought down, yet all along he remains profoundly exposed and under attack. So tragedy is a foreclosure of the tragic; it offers an answer to the tragic question purely and simply in the form of an accentuated question. I would say that in tragedy man's "Why?" becomes deepened and darkened into a "Why not?"

Although the tragic is not precisely tragedy, we may learn much about the tragic by considering how it becomes explicit and controlling in formal tragedy. First, observe that in tragedy the victim is at the same time a hero, not unlike a hostage who, by being chosen for this singular bout with destiny, assumes unwittingly a substituting or vicarious role. He takes the slings and arrows of outrageous fortune in our stead. Regarding him, we think, "There but for the grace of God go I." Indeed, it almost seems that by virtue of being caught within the tragic maelstrom the hero-victim has been singled out from ordinary mortals, set apart for special if sardonic honor. This is plainly true of Oedipus or King Lear or Electra; it is no less true of people off the stage who have been summoned to a similar meeting. And it remains true even if the person involved has lost every vestige of individual allure or command. How often has a Christian minister come to offer his sympathy and left with an undeniable feeling of dignity and respect! There is a strange greatness even in man's wretchedness which classic tragedy makes clear.

Secondly, observe how tragedy interprets the tragic as taking place at the outer limits of man's comprehension and competence. In this perspective, more perhaps than any other, "all the world's a stage." Our destiny appears to be contained within ever-encroaching boundaries. Life is a trap, a treadmill, and a torment. In tragedy the tragic is never merely accidental or coincidental; it has the look of something foreordained, decided in advance, decided against man's fulfillment. To be sure, tragedy may include an element of sheer contingency or chanciness—brief encounters, dropped handkerchiefs, wrong turnings, unwitting disclosures, and the rest—but these serve more as theatrical conventions or stage whispers than as the solid and substantial movement of the tragic. They only render the tragic momentum in dramatically plausible terms. They are minor details within a major pattern of necessity which they both illustrate and body forth.

From this, in the third place, it is but a short step to a view of life that sees man as in a state of siege, beset behind and before by a destiny which has turned back upon him with implacable, destroying force. As the tragic becomes modeled into tragedy, it approaches the conception of doom or fate. From this point of view it does not greatly matter whether human existence is seen as a dangling over nothingness or as a containment in nothingness, since both spell fatal necessity for man.

Why is it therefore that the tragic sense of life is never simply or solely fatalistic? Because in every human situation two forces are at work, not one, forces indicated by the words "fulfillment" and "frustration," which were used earlier. To return to Jaspers' way of speaking, human breakdown and defeat significantly reveal the true nature of things; they demonstrate that "reality is split and truth divided" so that "Being itself has a crack running through it." [4] Though tragic man is up against the universe, or reality, or Being itself, it is not true that Being is altogether against man. For does not man draw from Being the very strength by which he either resists or submits to its decree? So too Paul Tillich, writing from within the Christian faith, has shown that the tragic sense includes awareness of this fundamental rift or cleft in reality, not merely that between man on the one side and reality on the other.[5]

The arresting truth thus expressed is that the same reality which fulfills also frustrates, and this truth may just as well be put the other way round. As Jaspers says, "There is no tragedy without transcendence . . . when man faces the tragic, he liberates himself from it. . . . This is a movement toward man's proper essence,

---

[4] *Ibid.*, p. 94.

[5] See especially *Systematic Theology*, I, 188, 232.

which he comes to know as his own in the presence of his doom." [6]
This warning in Jaspers against absolutizing the tragic, isolating
it as nothing-but-tragedy, must be heeded. However closely tragedy
approaches fatalism, it is never quite identical with it.

According to Jaspers this movement in man toward liberation
is not caused by any providential release coming from beyond the
tragic, but takes place within the tragic and through its own power.
It means standing fast amidst shipwreck so that knowing my own
extremity becomes my very means of overleaping it—a doctrine proclaimed long before by thinkers of more explicit religious persuasion
such as Kant, Pascal, or Augustine. There is, however, a decided
difference between Jaspers and the Christian thinker on this point.
It consists in the fact that the liberation of which Jaspers writes is
necessarily self-liberation, and the only possible transcendence of
the tragic is for him self-transcendence, despite his frequent protestations to the contrary. Jaspers' tragic man bears more resemblance
to Nietzsche's "superman" than Jaspers himself seems willing to
admit.

Just here lies the sharp distinction which must be made between Jaspers' existential humanism and the Christian faith he rejects with unfeigned but resolute regret. It is not, as he wrongly
claims, the difference between a tragic humanism and an untragic
Christianity. Rather, it is that between two entirely contrary under-
standings of the final trust upon which human life is to be founded;
it is a question of the last court of appeal. For Jaspers the tragic
stage is set within the boundless reaches of the "Encompassing"
with its "symbolic ciphers" and ultimate "silence." But for the
Christian tragic happenings occur within the vast design and mighty
purpose of God's providence.

This does not mean at all, as Jaspers supposes, that to the Chris-

[6] *Op. cit.,* p. 41.

tian such untoward and malevolent events as deserve the name tragic cease to be so or are idealogically transmuted into something better and more bearable. For the believer as well as for the agnostic, there are things which have to be faced, struggled with, and fashioned into the structure of human existence. What is more, they are indubitably tragic things. The real difference, to put it bluntly, is that the Christian believer finds and thus affirms the strength for this engagement with the tragic not in himself but in his God. From the Christian point of view, therefore, it is truer to say that man is himself transcended in the presence of the tragic than that he surmounts or transcends the tragic by virtue of being simply what he is. In Christian faith the tragic principle is not side-stepped but is actually incorporated into the providential principle in such a way that the tragic is not removed but genuinely resolved.

III

What is the character of this Christian resolution of the tragic? In answering this question, our discussion with Jaspers must be carried to a deeper level where we may expect to find the issues sharpened against a background of growing consensus. In this spirit we can accept his warning, mentioned above, that tragic knowledge must not be warped into a rationalistic scheme in which its intrinsic polarity is lost. Jaspers rightly says: "In the original vision, tragedy and the release from it are linked together. But if we rob tragedy of its opposite pole and isolate it as nothing-but-tragedy, we fall into a bottomless chasm where none of the great tragic compositions have been built." [7]

This temptation to generalize exclusively on the basis of the tragic is certainly avoided in all great imaginative and reflective works. While accepting the fact that our existence is undoubtedly

[7] *Ibid.*, pp. 100-101.

tragic, they do not pretend that it is nothing-but-tragedy. By formalizing the tragic into tragedy, they do not by the same token absolutize it. By refusing to take this further step into a schematizing ideology, such works as Shakespeare's *Hamlet* or Unamuno's *The Tragic Sense of Life,* for example, preserve within what is tragic something of its own original and native quality; they are in a quite exact manner true to life.

Once having agreed with Jaspers to this extent, however, we must go on to inquire whether his conception of polarity within the tragic is the only valid one. Such release or transcendence as he discovers here is in fact no more than an interminable questioning, despite his word "liberation." It cannot possibly be a true deliverance, for it has, he says, "an uncommitted, hovering character. . . . We must not clamor for explanations of whatever has been, will be, and always is, but we must listen for that which is trying to speak to us." [8] All that Jaspers offers, then, is room to breathe, a place to stand on a sinking ship, the right to ask a question that must not expect an answer.

But may not this questioning itself be questionable? On this basis can Jaspers ever understand aright the bent and bearing of man's tragic inquiry? In Christian faith, at all events, it is certainly no mere "clamor for explanations" but something that probes deeper and reaches further. It is an appeal to God to justify his ways with men. That is clearly the inflection, if not the very grammar, of every agonized and perhaps ironical "Why?" that is wrenched by tragic visitations from men and women; and it is by no means the exclusive property of believers in God either. As an agnostic philosopher Jaspers cannot understand or grant this. Since he does not want God brought into the tragic picture at all, he cannot really grasp the significance of what is tragic. By insisting that

[8] *Ibid.,* p. 103.

the tragic question is identical with its own answer, he simply identifies release with the very situation from which release is sought.

Now Jaspers is par excellence the philosopher of openness, going far beyond even Bergson in this respect. He will not, he says, foreclose issues or freeze reality into any categorical mold. This is all very well, but let us not confuse such openness with either transcendence or deliverance from the tragic, since it dissolves the very polarity which Jaspers wishes to maintain. Indeed, his preference for openness and suspense, his commitment to the uncommitted, rules out altogether and in advance the possibility that through the tragic God may be trying to speak to us.

We may challenge Jaspers at yet another point. Do words such as "inclusion" or "transformation" convey at all adequately what happens to the tragic in the perspective of our faith? Evidently he means them to refer to Christian thought processes, certainly not to the action of God. He seems to have in mind a kind of ideological alteration by which believers deal with the tragic as if it were really something else, indeed something already very different, not tragic at all but in fact providential and gracious. Although he is too polite to say so, Jaspers is in effect charging us with unreality and illusionism. He feels that we are too weak to stand the full weight of the tragic and are compensating for that weakness by the doctrine of Providence, among other things.

That would be bad enough if it were true; but it is not, at any rate as a general truth derived from the classic expressions of our faith. By and large, Christian documents and practices fail to reveal any such ideology; and where it does put in an appearance in some cult or other, it stands condemned by the main stream of Christian testimony. To be inspired by faith in God is not to be excused from the requirements of plodding patience, stubborn courage, or daily fidelity. And the doctrine of Providence in particular has always had to presuppose the tragic—all the "vast nothingness and self-destruction in this world" of which Jaspers rightly speaks. Surely it is a rule of faith, no less than logic, that only what is first admitted and acknowledged can be actually included or transformed.

But words such as "inclusion" and "transformation," whatever their intent, have the effect of making faith seem simpler and easier than it actually is. Since they come from outside faith and constitute a negative appraisal of faith, they seem strikingly at variance with what takes place within faith. They simply do not ring true; they do not describe us as we are or life as we know it to be. Christianity does not afford to those who believe in Providence the kind of untragic security which men like Jaspers impute to it. Even the most durable and resilient Christian is not in the habit of descrying automatically, as by a reflex of the soul, a divine purpose hidden beneath every tragic happening.

Let us go still further. Belief in Providence may actually be harder for Christians than for non-Christians, who perhaps do not expect so much from God. It may well be more difficult to believe in the absence of God than not to believe in the existence of God, like Jaspers. For although one may trust ultimately that God reveals himself by silence and absence no less than by his word and presence, such a trust is just as likely to be thwarted as confirmed by really tragic visitations. More than straining our credulity merely, the tragic throws our entire Christian existence into jeopardy by making questionable the goodness and power of God. So, far from having a pat answer ready which annuls the tragic, faith in God is sorely tried and tested by the tragic.

Again, must we not ask whether Christians do not see the tragic as a forcing of God's hand and therefore plead with him to vindicate himself? Surely Jaspers is wrong in holding that the tragic experience involves "no accusation, only lament." Quite clearly, one cannot accuse a being in whom one does not believe; but such an accusation becomes altogether possible when belief is actively present, as every reader of the books of Job and Jeremiah must know. Yet the man of faith is unwilling to let God go even when he feels that God has abandoned him; and it is just this sense of abandonment which makes the tragic really, undeniably tragic for the believer. It is worse to be forsaken than to be merely frustrated. Quite as much as the nonbeliever the believer too is well acquainted with whatever is monstrous and malevolent in existence and makes no pretense of being immune from it. He even lays the tragic to God's charge, saying words like these: "Though he slay me, yet will I trust in him," or, "Nevertheless not my will, but thine, be done."

One wonders in fact whether in the whole range of world literature there can be found a single example of unrelieved or undeserved misfortune where the question of transcendent justice is not raised within and by the very situation which apparently denies it. Can we actually comprehend, say, Racine's *Phèdre* or Aeschylus' *Prometheus Bound* solely in terms of the tragic principle? No, for on the contrary these and other tragedies make bold to enter into argument with a higher power of Being from which, or rather from whom, a justifying and delivering word is sought. Indeed, the entire history of dramatic tragedy may be said to consist in an immemorial dispute of man with God. Here it is as if the tragic could not even be set forth without some sort of muted and provisional avowal, a recognition, however grudging or complaining, of the truly providential. Just because it is Providence which is being questioned by the tragic, it is impossible for the tragic to make answer simply by repeating itself.

It was said a few pages back that in Christian faith the tragic principle is taken up into the providential principle in such a way that the tragic, while certainly not removed, is genuinely resolved. Now we are in better position to understand this. Stated a bit differently, the providential and the tragic are not two contradictory ideologies between which every serious thinker has to make a choice; they are instead major and minor principles within our total faith-perspective. So where Jaspers speaks of a noetic act or authentic awareness whose very question is its own answer, Christians speak of a schooling of desire and will to take whatever comes from God, of a prayerful obedience no matter what he sends us. No ideational sleight of hand or artificially induced optimism, but a putting of the major and minor principles into their proper place, is what is here demanded. For it is obvious that if there is nothing in existence which makes the tragic possible, there is likewise nothing which makes Providence necessary. Can there be any thought of Providence as the guiding, guarding, governing love of God which does not have to reckon with the fact that there is that in being which needs to be kept under control, against which I must be protected, through and beyond which I have to be led?

The conception of Providence which has been growing in these chapters is far indeed from any sort of divine regimentation of events or any dictatorial planning of human destiny. Rather, we have acknowledged the rigidities of history, the inexorable passage of time, the power of human freedom, the arbitrary look of fatality, and the anxious ambiguity of day-to-day existence to go counter to God's gracious will. But these have been acknowledged not merely because they pose questions for a Christian understanding of the Providence of God, but even more because they make that understanding both necessary and possible.

There can be no doubt, however, that the faith we profess puts its fundamental emphasis elsewhere than upon the tragic. Jaspers is right; there is polarity in the tragic. But it is not an internal complication only; it derives its character from a connection which is maintained between God and his created world. It is not purely situational but relational. I may agree with Emily Dickinson that

> I like a look of agony,
> Because I know it's true.[9]

Yet why is it true, and what is true about it? Agony is not a simple but a remarkably complex feeling, even more so than physical pain. There is polarity or tension in agony, struggle as well as surrender, proud reluctance no less than humble endurance, and all of these together—remember Samson, remember the Laocoön. Yes, there is always something more to be said than that life is tragic, and precisely because this too must be said.

What is the nature of this "something more"? Lately it has become the theological fashion to put the case for Providence by asserting that there is also, in addition to much that is tragically evil in the world, a benign and supervening God. First one must show that he is utterly realistic and can look unwelcome facts in the face; afterward he may allow himself to speak out on behalf of Christian faith. Is this perhaps what lies behind the idea that Providence, in Gerhardt Kittel's words, is the "great Nevertheless" or, in Tillich's words, an "in spite of"? Reduced to simplest terms, this way of developing the doctrine of Providence goes something like this. You begin by doggedly enumerating all the things that threaten to undo God's saving purpose in the world, giving them some sort of rationale in tragic or pseudo-tragic terms, but then add triumphantly, as by an inspired afterthought: "This, however, is not the whole of the matter. There is something in being which fights against frustration and for our fulfillment; let us call it God, or Providence."

I may have caricatured this position slightly yet not, I think, unfairly. The point is that here the nature of what lies beyond the tragic is specified exclusively with reference to the tragic; God, therefore, is one who says No to the tragic, and so must we in

---

[9] Used by permission of Little, Brown & Co.

God's name. Our thought moves in only one direction, from the tragic to the providential.

Now I submit in all candor that this theological surrealism will not do. Actually and characteristically, our Christian faith moves in the opposite direction—from affirmation toward questioning, from belief in a God who is mighty to save toward doubt of the supremacy of what is tragic over us. That is surely the movement of the apostle Paul's declaration that nothing in all creation can separate us from the love of God in Christ, to take a classic and decisive illustration. The apostle speaks about the tragic from the vantage point of a faith which knows what lies beyond, and indeed above, the tragic. He already stands by faith on the other and affirmative side of any "nevertheless" which he might utter in the teeth of the tragic. It is abundantly clear that Paul affirmed the sovereign concern of God for men not as an added thought nor as a dialectical counterweight but as the ultimate and therefore prior conviction which inspired his refusal to take the tragic at face value in the first place.

It remains true that the tragic can be embraced and overcome only if it is admitted into the doctrine of Providence. But we can see now that although its admission is basic to the doctrine, it is hardly central. A Christian sees the tragic from the standpoint of the providential, not the providential from the angle of the tragic. He thus discovers its place within a wider, deeper frame of reference, so that the tragic does not write its own ticket or plead its own cause. Our faith articulates the keen sense that all life must be lived "here below" and therefore needs the sustenance and staying power of God who is "there above."

Thus it follows that Christians believe in a God who may say Yes as well as No to what is tragic. Only so can faith's own "nevertheless" issue from the awareness that we are kept and stayed by a Love revealed not simply in spite of but within, through, and because of tragic destiny. In George Herbert's compact words,

> This is the famous stone
> That turneth all to gold;
> For that which God doth touch and own
> Cannot for less be told.

IV

The Christian faith draws its strength and sanction for meeting the tragic in life from the cross of Jesus Christ. It is the cross that gives Christianity an undeniable point of contact with every tragic fact or meaning, yet by the same token our faith is radically distinguished from any view of life that is only tragic.

Who among us would want to claim that the cross is not tragic? That opinion is possible only to nonbelievers such as Karl Jaspers, who has no hesitation in declaring that in Jesus Christ "man takes his cross upon himself" so that while Christ is the "deepest symbol of failure in this world, yet he is in no sense tragic. In his very failure he knows, fulfills, and consummates." [10] There is much that is true in this statement, especially as regards Christ's victory achieved through failure. But there is also something false. On such an interpretation the cross means the way in which man himself, by simply going out to meet what is tragic, is able to take it to himself, neutralize, and transcend it. I am strongly tempted to suggest that here man becomes his own psychiatrist in Christ. Salvation on these terms has all the earmarks of a process of sublimation.

While not wishing to deny for a moment that psychiatry may shed light on the Atonement, we are bound to point out that in Jaspers' view there is not the slightest hint that God acts through the cross to reconcile men to himself. Neither is there any hint that

[10] *Op. cit.*, p. 40.

Jesus bore the cross in obedience to God's holy will rather than out of Herculean courage and compassion for his fellow sufferers. On Jaspers' view there is justice done to the human, representative, vicarious aspect of Christ's work, to be sure; but what is missing is precisely what Christians believe most firmly and distinctively about the cross. We proclaim that the cross is actually crucial for God as well as for mankind. Our Lord's death does not serve some hidden, ulterior purpose but is wedded to the plain working of God's love disclosed through his beloved Son. Far more than merely the result, the cross is the most powerful revelation of that love.

Now why does Jaspers wish to evacuate God from the one event that reveals God most centrally to the eyes of Christian faith? Why should he insist upon viewing the cross in terms of the tragic hero and not of the suffering servant? Why, indeed, does he retain this particular symbol at all? It can only support his thesis by being robbed of the very meaning which faith finds in it. Only because the cross, that tragic burden, has its focal place within the mysterious economy of God, can it be thought to bring about even the sort of salvation which nonbelievers seek to attribute to it. Jaspers refuses the providential in order to affirm the tragic, but we Christians do not refuse the tragic for the sake of believing in the providential. Recall Charles Kingsley's simple, heartfelt prayer: "Teach us by thy cross, that however ill the world may go, the Father so loved us that he spared not thee."

How strange it is that the cross of Christ should seem so much less tragic to unfaith than it does to faith! That God so loved us that he spared not Jesus is exactly the message of salvation as we Christians understand and declare it. We believe that the cross is a channel of grace for men and women only because it represents a tragic necessity for God. We believe that the cross is the lifting up of man only because it is the bending down, indeed in some sense the humiliation, of Almighty God. We believe that for our salva-

153

tion it was utterly necessary for God to stoop so low and to put himself at man's disposal, even at man's mercy, by giving up his own Son. Thus at the heart of this awesome event there is something very like sacrifice and suffering, required of God by man's stubborn continuance in ways of sin. By the cross God proved once for all that he is in dead earnest with us and made good his claim to be the Lord of life and death, of heaven and hell.

If it is not tragic that God should need to become involved as one of us in costly pain and heart-wrenching loss, what else in all existence can be called tragic? Yet the cross is tragic just because it is so truly providential. For upon the cross God himself "took her infirmities, and bare our sicknesses" (Matt. 8:17 K.J.V.). It was necessary in Sir James Baillie's words "for a completely divine life to pass through the ordeal of all nature's conditions, and to do this in the very worst form possible, so as to prove the entire dominion of spirit over nature, to show the exaltation of spirit in and through its very humiliation." [11] The tragic things in this world are not absorbed and sublimated by man; they are entered into and taken up by God. Here we come as near as we are likely to come to the very crux and heart of the Christian gospel.

For the cross, it must always be remembered, is the climax of the entire moving in of God upon and through our earth-bound, fretful life. It is prefigured in the humble birth of the incarnate Lord; thus Orthodox theologians have seen in the mysterious gifts brought by the wise men ointments for Christ's burial. And it is not until the Resurrection that the whole meaning of the cross is made plain. For the Resurrection does not disclose some new and unexpected factor, some secret weapon turning the tide of tragedy into a triumphal march; it sets forth the truth that on the cross God's victory over sin and death is conclusively won.

[11] *Reflections on Life and Religion* (London: George Allen & Unwin, Ltd., 1952), p. 67.

What the cross teaches us, therefore, is that Providence is not only the contradiction but even more the utilization of the tragic. What is saved must be entered into and taken up. What man accepts must be acknowledged by God. By the cross whatever is truly tragic is rendered serviceable to the design of Providence. And in order for this to happen, God must take the form of a servant, since as Dietrich Bonhoeffer wrote from prison, "Only a suffering God can help." Thus God achieves the providential resolution of everything tragic. Perhaps it does not matter too much whether we call the cross tragic or providential, as it is so clearly both together.

In conclusion, what should be our Christian response to those tragic visitations that menace our security and safety in the world? Gabriel Marcel has said somewhere that "at the back of hope lies some sort of tragedy." That is a true word. It is not enough to be those for whom Christ died; we are to be those in whom he lives. More than an inheritance, faith is also a promise. And one sure sign of this livingness of faith is the assurance that the tragic, if and when it comes, can be accepted at the hands of God. The disciple, after all, is not above his Lord.

This acceptance, furthermore, is neither stoic resignation nor existentialist revolt. Rather, it is making virtue out of necessity, which the apostle Paul called glorying in our infirmities and weakness. Providence is seen most plainly when it upholds us in the midst of our fragility and frailty. We could never know, much less return, God's sovereign concern unless we also knew ourselves to be expendable and perishable, unless we could find cause to glory in our vulnerable and dangerous existence. These are the very means by which God moves and acts to reconcile us with himself.

Somebody once observed that the "most real thing in life is death, the most real thing in joy is pain." These words are not untrue, and yet there is a higher and a sterner truth. A Christian believes that there is a joy that seeketh us through pain and a life that breaks the bonds of death asunder. For us, therefore, there is but one sadness; and that is not to be saints.

Paul, who gave the Christian doctrine of Providence its charter, also declared the sum and substance of the Christian response to what is tragic. "Troubled on every side, yet not distressed; . . . perplexed, but not in despair; persecuted, but not forsaken; cast down, but not destroyed; always bearing about in the body the dying of the Lord Jesus, that the life also of Jesus might be made manifest in our body." (II Cor. 4:8-10.) So Paul expressed both man's tragic realization and God's providential resolution. We live by the conviction that in front of every sort of tragedy lies hope. There is the Easter message in a single sentence. If God be for us, who indeed can be against us?

7

Technics and Vocation

"O Lord, let us not live to be useless; for Christ's sake. Amen."
—*John Wesley*

No effort to restate the meaning of Providence in our own day can afford to neglect the role of technical development in modern civilization generally. It goes without saying that this is a very large and complicated subject upon which no one can presume to have the last word. But as Pastor Lauriol of Paris remarked, if it were enough to grant the difficulty of a problem in order to solve it, every dunce would be a graduate in mathematics. Furthermore, we do the cause of Christ no real and reasonable service if we merely tend to confirm people in what they suspect already, that our faith is sadly out of touch with the kind of life they know best. Obviously it is quite impossible to bear a Christian witness before the world without having to reflect earnestly and critically upon those forces which give to the world its indubitable, telling shape.

There is a further motive for dealing with this whole area which more closely concerns the task of Christian theology itself. After all, technics is man's way of planning and attempting to control the course of his own life. Providence, on the other hand, is God's way of designing and directing that same life. Hence to raise the question about Providence is to ask whether it is complementary or contradictory to human technics. Is God's will truly carried and realized within the structures and operations that are typical of present-day society? Does the contemporary shape of things show God at work, and is it pliable to his purpose as our faith declares it? And if a Christian asks the question about technical civilization, he approaches the same set of issues from the nearer end. Does man's amazing capacity for manipulating and organizing, for technical "know-how" and "follow-through," really body forth God's intention for his world? Or does it, rather, stand in God's path, possibly even thwarting and confounding his plan for bringing mankind into saving fellowship with himself?

As everyone is aware, this latter sort of question has been among the most disquieting reflections of our self-styled atomic age. When natural forces and human science combine to form an unholy alliance in which, as Robert Calhoun has said, what seemed for a time to be our more and more obedient servants have put on the mask of destructive demons, we are duty bound to ask such uneasy questions. Have we perhaps been taking things too much into our own hands lately? May not all our shiny gadgetry have a more sinister and guilty meaning? Are we trespassing upon forbidden territory with our technology?

The Christian must make such answer as he can in the light of his faith in the providence of God. Just what that faith should have to say about the inquisitive, inventive creature called man, and particularly about his vocation under God in a civilization like ours, is a matter which concerns us all both profoundly and inescapably. For what is at stake here, once again, is nothing less than the character of God's concern for man's being in the world.

I

For the last hundred years or so a lively debate has been going on regarding the effect of technics upon human worth and welfare. By and large, it has subjected our so-called machine age to a lot of negative criticism, in which Christian thinkers have often joined enthusiastically. The machine, in fact, has been pointed to as the source if not the actual cause of almost all the ills that modern flesh is heir to—economic depression, the weary cycle of wars cold or hot, social upheaval, even personal disintegration. The machine has had its champions, too, but they have been well-nigh snowed under by the avalanche of gloomy protest. From Thoreau and Ruskin to Georges Bernanos and Philip Wylie the verdict against machine civilization has been pretty much the same. It is making a thing, a tool, a dupe of man. Probably Emerson, the sage of Concord, put the indictment as pithily as anybody else:

> Things are in the saddle,
> And ride mankind.

As Christians have lent their support to this charge, they have proclaimed the "dignity of the individual" and the "sacredness of human personality." And yet these well-intentioned slogans, which were fighting words to an older generation, have already begun to wear shockingly thin. What has happened to them? The trouble with them is not so much that they are untrue as that they have lost their bite, their cutting edge of Christian relevance. A great deal has been taking place since Thoreau built his shack on Walden Pond and Ruskin enjoyed his mornings in Florence. The rapid current of technology has carried us all far downstream. Now there is literally no place to hide. No longer can we counter the ascendancy of the machine simply by lodging literary or sermonic complaints against the machine.

Naïve and frightened as it now seems to have been, the anti-machine mentality could only avoid coming to grips with basic issues. For as the machine became the accepted symbol of inhumanity, it was easy to forget that man alone is able thus to dehumanize himself. A curious instance of this fact is found in recalling that

Frankenstein, in Mary Shelley's novel of that name, first meant a man destroyed by his own invention but soon came to mean the destroying robot itself. Hence the machine became the villain of the piece. There even grew up a plausible sort of modern myth— the myth of the robot that walks and talks and may even think like a man. It was understandable enough, this anti-technological folklore; but it was mainly a panic reaction.

Only quite recently has it begun to appear that man himself, not his mechanical contrivances, is the root of the difficulty. If the machine threatens to supplant man, it is because man has been assuming more and more machine-like qualities. To this entire development the words of an Old Testament psalm are vividly applicable:

> They have mouths, but do not speak;
>   eyes, but do not see.
> They have ears, but do not hear;
>   noses, but do not smell.
> They have hands, but do not feel;
>   feet, but do not walk;
>   and they do not make a sound in their throat.
> Those who make them are like them;
>   so are all who trust in them. (115:5-8 R.S.V.)

Though the writer is plainly thinking of graven images, it would be foolish to suppose that these words are irrelevant to our own technically dominated society. As the tool becomes an idol, its makers become its servants. Yes, our highly valued techniques have clearly been technicizing us, devaluing us in our own eyes because of the trust we put in them.

Technics began, as every student of anthropology knows, with the extending and refining of human capacities. The wheel was a better foot, the lever a stronger arm, the telescope a keener eye. All the arts and crafts, in fact, signified that "Man is the master of things," though probably not in quite the sense in which the poet Swinburne used that confident, ardent phrase. The story of man's technical prowess is a very long one; until about a century and a half ago it was a slow uphill climb. Then a sharp upward curve is noticeable; an astounding accumulation and acceleration of technics occurs. Some of us, not unnaturally, are beginning to wonder if this curve has not turned back already on itself, tending to become a vicious circle. We may summarize this boomerang process by saying that man is now being remade by the very things he makes. Consider, for instance, the words used today to describe personal wholeness and social harmony: "adjustment" and "contact," lifted out of the repair shop; "integration," "factor," and "manipulation" —this last the most horrendous of all, coming out of the sciences —and many, many more of the same. These metaphors reveal as much about us as about our tools. All are borrowed from the technical realm and applied without apology or excuse to human beings. They bespeak a fearful metamorphosis of persons in our time. Just several decades ago Robert MacIver could define culture as what we have and civilization as what we use, but we can draw no such line today. Now culture simply means civilization, for the things we use are in fact using us. We are caught in a kind of projection backward, or an inverse intentionality, as we take on the protective coloration of our own devices. In every exposed corner of our being we are increasingly subject to what Gabriel Marcel precisely terms "techniques of degradation."

And this is bound to happen whenever technics ceases to be man's way of extending himself and becomes instead his way of exalting himself. Perhaps it is a paradox, but the root of our self-debasement to the tool level is exactly our idolatrous technical pride. Sooner or later he who exalts himself will be humbled—we have the gospel's word for it—and who will deny that we have been humbled no less than frightened by the terrible things our brains and hands have lately been devising?

There are many people in our time, both East and West, who seem altogether unwilling to accept this truth. They shut their eyes to what has now become a commonplace fact, that modern technics through the assertive logic of its own specialization makes the goals for which it was first intended more and more inoperative and seemingly irrelevant. Hence it is a distinguishing trait of technical society that all its difficulties should be regarded as "purely technical" and handed over to expect technicians for solution. This is one of those assumptions which are embedded so deeply in our way of life that they are all but hidden. Even the arts have not escaped its pervasive influence. Manual dexterity, virtuosity, or stylistic expertness is widely prized above feeling depth, personal dedication, or evocative arousal. However, this assumption is terribly if not indeed tragically false. It was Peter Drucker who pointed out that mass production itself is not a merely technical but a social principle, made possible only through mass organization founded upon imitation and consent.

This brings us to the relationship of means to ends in technical civilization, a subject on which some truth and much foolishness have been written. Whatever its failings, the robot mythology was right in posing the issue between mechanical means and human ends. Yet its adherents seldom grasped the fact that technical development amounts to much more than a simple displacement or transfer of human "functions." It means the general abdication or self-disfranchisement of human beings bent on exploiting nature but discovering that they themselves were being exploited. Means, after all, do not change themselves into ends; they are given that importance by the kind of trust men put in them. Where trust in technics becomes inordinate and unwarranted, there men must correspondingly faint and fail. In our own day this kind of confidence has become presumptuous to the point where we have every right to ask theological questions about it.

What is at stake here is the way in which *homo faber* becomes himself a fabrication, the producer a product, the artisan a seeming artifact. In light of this how shall a Christian thinker proceed? Instead of setting up a sharp antithesis between man and the machine, as in the older view, we have to raise the much profounder question about man's own image of himself. Who does he think he is? This is by no means a simple question. The human image which has been forming under the impetus of technics is not at all clear. On the contrary, it is saddled with the ambiguity and equivocation which are betrayed in everything that pertains to man.

Then let us say, for we must, that all aspects of our technicized existence spell out this *double-entendre* in man's own being. From clock to cobalt bomb that which pays tribute to our ingenuity and dignity is also what threatens to debase if not to supplant us. Far more than a standing predicament this is a really tragic self-contradiction. Our advancing technical power brings in its wake decreasing human purpose, yet through this same power our purpose has to be exerted and realized.

Let us take a concrete illustration. Here is a man who loves good music and has gathered together a fine collection of recordings. Listening to them, he finds, brings welcome relief from the cramping routines of a machinelike existence. Horizons are broadened, cloud banks lifted, avenues of beauty opened, spirit abundantly satisfied. So far, so good. But it is not long in our kind of world before a quite unpremeditated transformation occurs. The music lover's enjoyment depends more closely, hinges more completely, upon the mechanical systems which make it possible. So he buys only the most flawless records after hours of painstaking investigation and comparison. He must have the finest reproducing and amplifying units he can afford. He spends days in shopping for the latest devices, looking constantly for methods of improving his improvements. Doubtless he will say in self-defense that all this adds greatly to his pleasure, but the point is that his pleasure itself has undergone a radical change. Before, he was alive to the nuances in the music of Beethoven or Bartók; now, he is alert to the sheer physical flow of sound that carries and supports the music. Indeed, that which is aesthetically the most irrelevant provides him with the keenest delight. To some friends who drop in for an enjoyable evening he announces proudly in the middle of a record, "Listen carefully; this is where you can hear Toscanini breathing."

What has been going on in this man? We must say that what at first enhanced his appreciation has more and more become a substitute for it. Somewhere and somehow a technological corner has been turned. The listener has become an operator instead. Musical enjoyment has been changed into a very different kind of pleasure, that derived from successfully manipulating sound systems. Once again the world of technics has boomeranged back upon the realm of personal enrichment, stifling what it was designed to satisfy.

One might go on indefinitely documenting the point from other human areas and interests, such as power tools, filing systems, household budgets, even the ancient and honorable game of golf. We could speak of prefabricated housing, precooked foods, or predigested knowledge. Here, however, are a few samples which everyone recognizes: communities which have organized social service to the point where the most difficult matter of all is where to refer a client; colleges that spend far more money on administration and promotion than on books, teachers, and students; or churches that habitually confuse the running of religious programs with the coming of God's kingdom. All these, and many more, betray this bedeviling paradox of a kind of control which has less and less control over itself.

Of almost every good thing in human life it can be said that it could not exist without some degree of technical proficiency. A mother's love runs out into the operations of baking, mending, ironing, shopping; the worship of God is the fruit of architectural engineering, liturgical planning, choir rehearsing, and many other technically oriented activities. I shall try to do full justice to the positive contribution of technics a bit later on. But here the self-contradictory character of our present situation must be pointed out. The all-conditioning force of our technics is evidenced most clearly in our efforts to break away from it. We are, it seems, caught in the grip of the almighty "how." We talk of deepening the spiritual life in our churches; but it soon comes down to forming a new group, having more meetings, hiring a new expert, and building a new chapel. By the time a few of these things have been done, the original motive has become lost in the technical shuffle. After several experiences of this sort I am bound to ask just what kind of world it is in which I can effect my purpose only by nullifying it.

No wonder that the older dualisms of subject and object, value and fact, spirit and matter, ends and means, have long since ceased to throw real light on our contemporary situation. We cannot invest machines with responsibility for the present impasse, but neither can we call them blameless altogether. For it is not of machines only that we have to speak and think, objects inert and neutral in themselves; it is to machine technics that we must turn our attention. The main reason why the idea of the "purely technical" is false is that every machine is part of an intricate web of human involvement; and the technics related to it belong, so to speak, to the very syntax of society itself. So a machine becomes the portent and earnest of the will of its inventor, operator, and owner. To illustrate: A bomb is correctly termed an "infernal machine," which does not merely imply that it is a remarkably good means to a very bad end. The truth about a bomb is somewhat more deep-going. It can only be understood and dealt with in the realm of technics as containing in itself a "built-in" power for destruction which not even the most rigorous analysis can separate from the mindless automaton that carries and delivers that power.

A Christian word must also be spoken to the astonishing technocratic utopianism which still prevails in large segments of our civilization. Today technics has undoubtedly acquired a kind of messianic complex which is actually but the death rattle of the cult of progress. Standing before the atom smasher or the giant calculator in a university laboratory, one quite readily forgets that a tool is only a tool. Such ingenious devices as these, it is true, weave a fabric of illusion which it is very hard to shake off. They appear self-contained and self-explaining but are not really so. Hence they bear, as has already been said, an odd resemblance to the idols against which the Hebrew prophets spoke out; for they exert much the same fascination and compel a similar service. Already, however, this utopian mentality is taking on the character of hoping against hope. Hard-pressed and with its back to the wall, it repeats its credos in more fearful vein. Its idols are beginning to crumble and fall.

Why not, then, call every sort of technology a curse and go back to the spinning wheel, the three R's or whatever one takes as his nostalgic norm? Simply because there is no going back but only a way forward. It is indeed God's will that we should live in what is here and now. And one of the things we have to live with is the strangely equivocal character of everything man makes or operates, a character which derives basically from everyman himself. A further illustration, this time on a much grander scale, may help to make this clear. A number of careful studies have shown conclusively that there is a very close correlation in modern history between war and mechanization. Now no one likes war, not even those whom pacifists call militarists; but war has resulted in the Bessemer process for making steel, the standardization of parts, motorized transport, then aviation and radio communication, this last bringing on nuclear fission, television, and possibly the start of interplanetary travel. While nobody in his right mind would term these unmixed blessings, neither are they unmixed evils. They simply betray the general ambiguity inherent in technics and man alike. They show, in fact, that technology is neither inhuman nor antihuman but all too human.

It all comes down then to the truth that the technical paradox is but the human paradox over again. The old Adam is still here, streamlined now for what automobile advertisers call sleek maneuverability. The trouble with him is not simply that he is old but that he is Adam. In saying so, we are not handing over the matter to high-pressure evangelists for solution, nor are we excusing ourselves from the need for rigorous and thoroughgoing thought. We are simply reckoning with the fact which it has taken many centuries of technology to make clear that a tool is only as good or as bad as its maker and user, that no battery of techniques can secure man against his own inner ambivalence and ineptness. That lesson might have been learned long ago; it has to be learned now.

II

Can any way be found out of this vicious technological circle? Is it possible that this dilemma may have within it what we may call a fortunate ambiguity, that is, an opportunity for Providence?

A Christian reply will recognize that if we seem to be caught in a vicious circle, yet the circle is one which revolves around man. Technics may mean the suppression, but it is at the same time the expression, of human capacity and worth. Thus it is proper to inquire whether there may not be forces at work in our kind of world which are positive as well as perverse. And first of all, we must begin by reconstituting the true image of man. The likeness which modern technology has given is certainly not the classic Christian picture. It is almost as if man had been willing to be made over into a stereotype of himself, as he signed away his right to master what he had conceived and put into operation. More than a decade ago Lewis Mumford made a judgment that is still devastatingly accurate. He wrote:

Today our best plans miscarry because they are in the hands of people who have undergone no inner growth. Most of these people have shrunk from facing the world crisis and they have no notion of the manner in which they themselves have helped to bring it about. Into every new situation they carry only a fossilized self. Their hidden prejudices, their glib hopes, their archaic desires and automatisms— usually couched in the language of assertive modernity—recall those of the Greeks in the fourth century B.C. or those of the Romans in the fourth century A.D. They are in a power dive and their controls have frozen. By closing their eyes they think they can avoid a crash.[1]

If this judgment strikes home, as it surely does, it is not only because Mumford describes the sociological fact that in a technical society man is always out of date and out of step owing to the inner speed and outer pressures within such a society. It is also, and even more, because Mumford here suggests the Christian truth that Adam lives on in everyman with his familiar self-concealing, self-protecting devices. There is undoubted truth in the cultural-lag theory, but it rests upon another truth concerning man which is both deeper and higher than its own.

Yet this is only the beginning of what Christian faith has to say on this urgent subject. Man, we declare, is created in the image of God. If this means anything, it means resemblance, mutual recognition, something not too far from kinship. In short, the likeness which we bear to God is woven firmly into the fiber of our

[1] *The Condition of Man* (New York: Harcourt, Brace & Co., 1944), p. 422. Used by permission of Lewis Mumford.

being. We are God's "others," not his objects. And this is structural and elemental with man, not merely hereditary or vestigial. It defines who I am here and now.

Man, of course, is a creature and not the Creator; no Christian teaching is allowed to overlook that. But the point has been labored enough among the orthodox, and little good can come of repeating it except to those who have forgotten it. Bearing the image of God does not make us pint-sized gods, or carbon-copy gods, or vest-pocket editions of God. But it does make us the counterpart of God, called into existence and maintained in it by him who cares for us. What now needs saying is that man the creature is no mere artifact of God, no ready-made product, plainly not his receding echo in the world, and least of all his tool.[2] On the contrary, the image of God, the bodying forth of God within the created world, is man's own destiny and birthright; it is what God means and makes every one of us to be. And therefore the task bound up in this gift is that of becoming what I really am, of living out the meaning of my life.

Moreover, man's relation to the natural world takes its cue and character from his relation of likeness to God. So in the Genesis story of creation God says, "Let us make man in our image," and almost at once comes the command to the new creature to "replenish the earth, and subdue it." Then man is endowed with the power of naming and taming natural facts and forces; we may even say that both science and technology receive their divine authorization at the creation. All this follows from the fact that man is created like God. The world is made for man; this is God's announced intention for both man and the world.

Therefore the Christian approach to human technology can

[2] On this matter, I personally believe, the priestly tradition in the Bible is to be preferred to the prophetic, which lapses occasionally into speaking of man as the clay and God as the potter, and so on.

never be entirely negative and critical. Our deep and biblically based conviction is that God wills man to have dominion over nature, appropriating it wherever possible to his advantage and adjusting himself wherever necessary to its rigors and requirements. Technics belongs within the very prerogative of man as made in the image of God. This realm of plans and projects and procedures is not simply divinely approved but divinely ordained. Emil Brunner makes the intriguing suggestion that technics as a whole proceeds from the erect walk which is man's natural endowment among living creatures. Thus he can look God in the face. And he is called to transcend nature in this manner just because he is called to be Godlike.[3]

To this end, a Christian believes, God imparts something of his own initiative, strength, and foresight. He intends to share his lordship with mankind. For man to be a creature is at once to be creative—a maker who in his own turn and sphere endlessly refashions the world. Can human technics possibly be invested with a greater dignity or authority than this? When God makes man, he does not merely bring another fact into existence, nor does he only pay tribute to his own omnipotence. Rather, he causes one to be who is to act as God's deputy or delegate within the natural, finite order. He crowns man with glory and honor and puts all things under his feet, as the eighth psalm has it. Hence technics remains in principle the token of God's sovereign concern for man, a concern which even the word "love" can but haltingly suggest.

At just this point, however, the theologians' task becomes most difficult. We have to define this positive rapport between divine creation and human creativeness without seeming either to humanize God or to divinize man. We must not blur the ultimate distinc-

[3] *Christianity and Civilization* (New York: Chas. Scribner's Sons, 1949), II, 5.

tion between creation and creativity, as happens in the view of theistic naturalism. But neither must we become engaged, like some contemporary neo-orthodox thinkers, in finding singularly devious ways of avoiding the basic truth that man is created like his Creator with all the rights and privileges appertaining thereto. Let us simply say, then, that the making of man consists in the self-giving of God. Our creaturely creativeness means at least this—that God, by calling us to join with him in his mighty work, shares his power and wisdom with us.

One further warning seems in place at this particular juncture. Much current talk about the image of God *in* man would appear to mean that each of us carries around inside himself a little piece of divinity, though it is never put so crudely. But the bond between man and God is one of likeness only, not identity whether complete or partial. Nevertheless the likeness is a real one, not fictitious or contrived. And if the image is not a part of God, still less is it a part of man, even his noblest and highest part. It sums up all that human existence means in God's own sight. This may be better expressed artistically than theologically, as in Michelangelo's "Creation of Adam" in the Sistine Chapel, which embodies the truth that man is God's own "opposite number" in the kingdom of creation.[4]

Without stopping to refine our thought further, let us sum up its significance for a theology of technics. Two fundamental principles, rather like ground rules, have been emerging. The first is that *power over nature is abundantly man's*. In fact, our mastery over the environment in which we must make our way is ordained of God, structured into what it means to be human. We are even commanded to be resourceful, inventive, productive, provident. Not

[4] Throughout the present section I have been tacitly taking issue with those like Brunner who maintain that the "image" is not substantial, but only relational, in man. I believe the symbol expresses more than human responsibility to God—rather, the whole structure of our existence as God-given and God-directed.

only the Bible but the entire history of technics lines this out. All the characteristic features of modern technology—regularized time, increased mechanical efficiency, multiplying of goods and services, standardizing of performance and product, transfer of human skill to automatic tools, and growing collective interdependence—all this belongs within the intention and thus within the providence of God. For technics is anchored solidly in man's authentic likeness to his God, bestowed upon him at his very creation. To quote George Herbert once again:

> More servants wait on man
> Than he'll take notice of.
>
> .   .   .   .   .
>
> Man is one world, and hath
> Another to attend him.[5]

The second principle contained within the doctrine of God's image is that *power over man is decidedly God's.* By the same token that man is set over and above the natural order, he is absolutely distinguished from God. Both distinctions stand or fall together. It is often said that while man is amazingly adept with respect to nature, with regard to his own human nature he seems sadly incompetent. The truth in such a judgment is put incisively by Lewis Mumford: "In attempting to seize power man tended to reduce himself to an abstraction, or, what comes to almost the same thing, to eliminate every part of himself except that which was bent on seizing power." [6]

We can put this in more definitely Christian language, too. Technics by its very proliferation and intensification greatly encourages that self-negation of man which is the essence of sin. Man the sinner is a disfigured image, "a good thing spoiled." Thus when

---

[5] From "Man."

[6] *Technics and Civilization* (New York: Harcourt, Brace & Co., 1934), p. 31.

we hold that man is made in God's likeness, we do not play down the fact of sin but simply call it by its correct name—self-distortion, self-disfigurement, self-destruction. Sin resembles those mirrors sometimes seen at county fairs which by ingenious alternation of concave and convex surfaces make either gnomes or giants out of passers-by. Not even sin can take away from man his own *raison d'être,* for that is given him by God. And man cannot deny this image without at the same time affirming it, even in this back-handed fashion. Technics is not identical with sin; and yet in modern civilization sin is certain to take a technological form, as that is the form in which our living has to be done.

Quite often, underlying the lament heard in our time that man is able to control everything but himself, there is a Stoic and not a Christian emphasis. It is significant that Stoicism, not Christianity, made a virtue out of self-mastery. Indeed the whole drift of optimistic scientism and technocratic messianism, with their confidence that human nature can and should be brought more and more under scientific-technical control, bears ample witness to this neo-Stoic tendency. But a Christian reads the situation very differently. He knows that mastery over human nature is not an engineering job, that self-control is not an item on the social planner's agenda, but instead a venture of faith which comes alone by way of God's acknowledged lordship over all man's life.

In speaking thus we do not want to appear ungrateful to modern science and technology; we only wish to question the claims made on their behalf, their right to make us conform and react automatically to the forces they have let loose in the world. If they are to condition us, what is to condition them? The answer must surely be found in the heart of faith, that being viable and available to God which Marcel has so finely termed "disposability." Here is probably the soundest way of stating what God's image means to men and women in our time. It means that to be placed above nature

173

is also to be placed under God, and that both man and nature can serve God's purpose insofar as man remains *open upward* to him.

III

God takes a certain grave risk when he makes man in his own image—namely, the risk that his gift may become mishandled and misshapen. In other words, technical creativeness spells freedom; and it is freedom in man that gives leverage to both God and Satan.

As was said in an earlier chapter, to do or not to do is basically the same as to be or not to be. Back of the knife edge of decision lies the full weight of destiny. In simplest terms, then, freedom means *being myself;* and this is obviously impossible unless I am at liberty to go contrary to the God who makes me free. For when all is said and done, it is up to me to become what I am. My freedom under God must also be freedom before God, else it is not even freedom. And my ability to create may be used in noncreative ways, in which case the image of God is honored in the breach rather than in the observance.

Now this Christian teaching about freedom illuminates profoundly the present technological difficulties in which we find ourselves. For as we have seen, it is precisely man's dependent likeness to God which assures human domination over everything that is natural and technical. To put the same truth the other way around, it is God's sovereignty which is the only possible guarantee of man's own freedom. And in this sense all technological issues are at bottom theological.

No one, I believe, has thought through more carefully the relation of technics to freedom than Emmanuel Mounier, the first editor of the journal *Esprit* and leader of the movement known in France as personalism. He has written:

The creative decision, by breaking a chain of probabilities or fatalities, or braving an intimidating play of forces, has upset all calculation; it was taken in conditions of uncertainty and confusion, but it becomes the creative origin of a new state of order and intelligibility. The world progresses and man forms himself by this alone. No technical organization will ever replace it; on the contrary, the more technique we contrive, the more freedom of decision will be required of us. . . . The free man is the man to whom the world puts questions and who responds accordingly; he is the *responsible* man.[7]

What Mounier says here is important on at least two counts. It will strike many people as a totally foreign idea that technics does not supplant but in fact demands the constant, knowing exercise of human freedom; yet this accent restores needed Christian balance to our contemporary searchings of heart. And the corresponding conviction, that freedom always means responsibility, while more familiar, brings to the fore again a tonic and astringent truth which needs not so much exposition as rendition.

On the first point, ours is the kind of civilization in which every new technical advance calls immediately into play the flexibility of freedom, far from putting it to death. Thus the music lover is not doomed to become a gadgeteer, nor the housewife a drudge, nor the minister an errand boy. For this is not God's plan for them —a truth which is enforced by the very increase and acceleration of technics within the modern world. What has been happening does not always have to happen. The more techniques abound, the more alert and determined our freedom must become.

So to take a matter which is on the mind of everyone today, the release of atomic energy does not in itself presage the final incapacity of man but renders man capable and also accountable to a degree hitherto undreamed of. This is both a warning and a guiding beacon;

[7] *Personalism,* tr. Philip Mariet (New York: Grove Press, 1952), pp. 63-64.

it spells not only annihilation but also advantage, at one and the same time. Neither cynicism nor optimism can save us. The truth, being greater, corrects and covers both. That truth is this—that man is not meant or made to be at the mercy of his tools but to retain command of them through his God-given freedom, which is to be second in command to his own Maker, Sustainer, and Redeemer. Providence may well appear malevolent if we seek to take it into our own hands, playing at being God; but if we are rightly warned and wisely guided by these awesome explosions and mushroom clouds, future history will have a different, more gracious story to tell.

True, the more techniques we have, the greater is the chance of going wrong, of getting hurt, of being taken in. We had better heed the forebodings of a Robert Oppenheimer, the apocalyptic ironies of a George Orwell or an Aldous Huxley. But this risk, this chance, is just what human freedom means; and it always looks in more than one direction. Thus is brought home to us the Christian lesson that man is the intended master of things, as surely as God is the master of men.

And secondly, this is but to repeat that freedom and responsibility are the same thing. The report of the World Council of Churches, meeting in Evanston in 1954, observed how modern civilization has increasingly taken the control of economic affairs out of the sphere of "automatic responses," so that what formerly was thought of as the working of inexorable laws of supply and demand is now a complicated joint activity engaged in by groups of managers, workers, and public servants in a far more humane context of trusteeship and the common good. We therefore stand already on a new stage in economic policy making. The day of townhouses and sweatshops, of predatory buccaneers and rioting radicals, is plainly and I think providentially past. This is only one of many pertinent examples which could be given.

We ought to take Christian courage from the fact that the free man is also the responsible man. Here once again human ambiguity becomes divine opportunity. It is as if we were being forced to be free, made to become what we know ourselves in God's sight to be.

Technical mastery can never be a real substitute for Providence; and whenever that presumption is made, it results in the self-degradation of the men and women who are bemused by it. Precisely by placing upon human beings the burden of responsibility for its development, the realm of technics releases and requires the full degree of their freedom. It involves them by the same token in the sustaining and governing work of God himself. So true is this that the more man takes the control of life into his own hands, the greater becomes his actual dependence—though not, alas, his conscious reliance—upon God's ultimate control. The more we try to provide our own providence, the more we stand in need of the providence of God. The more we strain toward the limits of our competence and comprehension, expressed so exactly in the word "know-how," the more we actually become aware of what these limits are. Hence it is not technicians but savages who "care nothing for Providence," in Pascal's words. We have now come to a point which makes our wonted technological complacence seem but a kind of impotence, based upon delusions of grandeur and issuing in chronic jitters and nightmarish musings. Thus it becomes searchingly and savingly plain that technics is never merely technical but providential.

Such a realization as this helps us to define our true vocation under God. Actually, of course, we have been thinking of vocation all through this chapter. As God calls man into being at the creation, so he recalls man to his true being in the here-and-now of everyday existence. We have been working our way rather cautiously toward an affirmative answer to the question whether modern, technicized man is even able to bear such a call from God. Are we so trapped in our maze of procedures, so enmeshed in the tightening web of our projects, that Providence cannot possibly get a word in edgewise? It is high time to declare our conviction that deep within the very tempo and texture of technical civilization man is more than ever before subject to the "calling, recalling, and manifold renewed recallings" of the most-high God.

And vocation or Christian calling is a peculiarly personal and "special" mark of Providence. Indeed we cannot understand our calling apart from the conviction that we have a definite place within the sovereign concern of God. To him it is not an accident that we are what we are here and now, for it is he who has put us where we are. No sort of human work, however unrewarding, monotonous, or distasteful, lies outside God's scrutiny and judgment, just as no sort of work is without his sustenance and joy.

Even in a world like ours this holds true. Just because it is more difficult for us to find our place and keep it, that place must be found. What is more, it can and will be found if we but learn to put our trust in Providence. Such trust, let it be granted, is not easy for us; and yet it can be learned because it must. Let us remember, too, that this is no vaguely "religious" or "devotional" matter but a deliberate and disciplined way of acting which has some specific directives. One of these concerns the personal self-realization of the worker through the energy and motive which he builds into his work; the other has to do with the contributive support which by his work he gives to others for the common good.

Every worker has the right to demand that the tasks assigned him should be such as to call forth his best initiative and to claim his finest effort. Vocation is not automation. In order to hear God's call on the job, a worker needs to be assured that his job can take what he has to give, that there is genuine correlation between its demands and his own powers. A kind of dynamic equilibrium between requirement and resource is what chiefly matters here; the point is that one should be able to find himself within his work. No one who is an occupational misfit can be expected to regard his work as his vocation in a Christian sense. This standard has but little to do with what goes by the name of security but much to do with day-to-day significance. Neither does it mean that there should be no drudgery at all in work, for every task has some aspects of drudgery about it. A teacher who fancies himself lecturing brilliantly before an admiring class of students soon discovers that much of his time is spent in grading papers and making out reports. And so it goes in everyone's line of work. But if a worker can realize himself in what he does, he can stand a great deal of chore work for the sake of a finished product which gives him the sense of personal fulfillment. All work is, or should be, eschatological in that it makes its end its beginning, its imperative its incentive.

The second mark of true vocation is that one's work should contribute consciously toward a more-than-private good. There is a precious togetherness in all work; but some is spurious or faked, like the honor that is said to exist among thieves or like the artificially induced sense of importance derived from the mere bigness of an enterprise in which one plays a tiny part. Yet surely there is a more genuine kind of loyalty to be found in doing one's job well—the determination not to let others down, the mutual confidence and solidarity and rapport which can and do make all working a co-working. What is at issue here is simply the principle, without which Christian vocation cannot exist, that the good of each of us is the good of all of us, so that work finds its true nature only as I make the common good my own. And let us note in passing that this principle has never been so clearly put before us as it has in modern technical society in which vocation becomes necessarily co-operation.

These vocational directives, clearly proclaimed and faithfully followed by Christian men and women in our technicized world, come to us from God. They place us under orders and define our tour of duty. Such a call, once heard and answered, is able to deliver us from a synthetic into an authentic mode of being, which ever after it is God's providential design to keep alive in us. We are summoned to do our work, whatever it may be, in creative, free, responsible existence. Thus man's true image reappears and is reconstituted. So God sets before us the promise that by not being conformed to this world we may prove—test out, search, *probare*—that which is his good and acceptable and perfect will for us. No longer do we need to scare ourselves, like children, with what our own hands have been making. Instead, we may accept the world of technics as a happier and more healthy omen, a sign of God's unfailing, self-imparting, endlessly resourceful fatherhood and lordship.

8

A Prayer-hearing God

"He who prays has his hand on the rudder of the world."
—John Chrysostom

The title of this chapter is borrowed from that of a sermon preached by Jonathan Edwards back in the year 1736 as an epidemic was raging in the neighborhood of Boston and a time of fasting and prayer was appointed by the churches in New England. It serves, I believe, as well as any other to catch up the meaning of our belief in Providence for that most personal and practical of Christian actions—praying. As Edwards told his congregation, God causes an "agreeableness" between our prayers and his providence. In other words, prayer is the correlate of Providence, as surely as man is the counterpart of God.

Prayer, then, is much more than another variation on the theme of Providence. It is the positive and inward grasping of that theme as it comes alive in believing people. Prayer is what we do about Providence and because of Providence. Hence they stand or fall together in the Christian life.

But there are difficulties involved in believing this. Some of the most familiar objections to praying arise in the conviction that God disposes and governs all things by his providence. Most ministers have had to deal with the same issue that was put to Origen of Alexandria in the third century:

It is reasonable that He who is the Father and Creator of the universe ... should dispense what is for the well-being of each one without being prayed to; just as a father does, who protects his little ones and does not wait upon their requests, either because they are unable to ask at all, or because through ignorance they often wish to receive things that are clean contrary to their profit and advantage. And we human beings are much further off from God than mere children are from the mind of their parents.[1]

Is not prayer made unnecessary in advance by Providence? Must it not be either superfluous or presumptuous? Why pray if God knows and attends to our needs before his help is even sought? If God is already disposed to care and to give, what may be gained by prayer? Is it not like holding a "farthing candle to the sun"?

In reply there are three things to be said. First, this drawback seems to come more from a rational wish for consistency between the action of prayer and the assumption on which it is based, than it does from any tension known and lived within the prayerful act itself. No doubt consistency is a virtue of which we can never have too much; but this objection to praying is surely more a perplexity than it is a predicament; and one suspects that even if it could be neatly answered, the actual practice of prayer would not be greatly changed or eased thereby.

Secondly, it can be pointed out that the same conviction about Providence which makes prayer seem difficult to some nevertheless makes prayer possible for all. Just think a moment: Could we ever meet this objection by *denying* that God provides for us? Would prayer become more likely if we were to assert that the Lord is *not* our shepherd, *not* the shade upon our right hand, *not* the keeper and restorer of our souls? Perish the thought! If it is true that belief

---

[1] *Library of Christian Classics* (Philadelphia: Westminster Press, 1954), II. Alexandrian Christianity, p. 248.

in Providence makes prayer puzzling sometimes, the same belief makes prayer reasonable always. There is, of course, a sense in which prayer has to take Providence pretty much for granted if it is ever going to begin, since I can hardly pray unless I believe or at least strongly surmise that God can give me what I ask him. Yet this is not to deny that there is another deeper sense in which prayer knows that Providence can never be taken *simply* for granted, or else there would be nothing really to pray for. Yet either way, we confront through prayer a realm of genuine mystery which cannot under any circumstances be rationalized and methodized. If Providence does not remove this mystery, at all events it does not aggravate it.

Thirdly, this objection that if God provides we have no need to pray is a curious mixture of truth and falsehood. Its truth consists in emphasizing the priority of God's concern to all our praying; that God's regard precedes and causes our response is in fact the presupposition of every honest prayer. But its falsity lies in trying to strait-jacket this rock-bottom conviction into a kind of theological fatalism which Origen has also stated for us:

First: if God knows the future beforehand, and it must come to pass, prayer is vain. Secondly: if all things happen according to the will of God, and if what is willed by him is fixed, and nothing of what he wills can be changed, prayer is vain.[2]

Such a forcing of the issue can only be called a masterpiece of overstatement. It simply identifies Providence with determinism. Here the word has lost entirely its meaning of "looking out for" and has been shut up in its other meaning of "seeing and planning ahead." It is as if the thought of God's care for us had been allowed to harden into that of his absolute control over us. Here is a sad

[2] *Ibid.,* p. 250.

confusion of faith's own profoundest assurance with the obiter dictum of a metaphysical finalism, against which theology must always be on its guard. And the confusion may be countered by showing, as has been done earlier, that we do not have to overstate our case for Providence in order to elucidate what Christians believe about the rapport between prayer and the prayer-hearing God.

All the same, this often-heard objection does have the real merit of exposing, though perhaps inadvertently, some genuine issues. These concern the Christian definition of prayer. While it has many modes and motives, prayer can be described most simply as "asking God for something." I think we must agree with Professor Farmer of Cambridge that if prayer is the heart of all religion, then petition is the heart of prayer. Most of the languages of the world appear to bear out this definition. Here the dictionary is certainly on the right track; prayer, it tells us, means "entreating, imploring, begging, beseeching, pleading"—all ways of asking God for something. Whatever more than this prayer may come to mean at the end, it can scarcely mean less than this at the beginning.

Seeing prayer from this petitionary angle, as I believe we must, does not involve us in the questionable business of trying to get God to change his mind or to alter the course of the world in our particular behalf. It is completely natural and proper that we should want to cast our cares on God in prayer, letting our sighs come before him and asking him to give us what we want or need as if our life depended on it—which it does. Yet it is quite another thing to try to cadge God's favors or cajole his good will for one's private advantage. In an old French chronicle there is this amusing prayer spoken by a commander before going into battle: "God, I pray Thee today to do for La Hire as much as Thou wouldst wish La Hire to do for Thee, if he were God and Thou wert La Hire." That little word "if" is what saves the prayer from crude and banal egoism; it introduces a humorously Christian note of modest reservation. At least La Hire recognizes that he and God are not exactly interchangeable. Without that note it is impossible to please God in our praying.

What prayer requires, then, is a certain "abandonment to Providence," as Catholic spiritual directors call it, which is nowhere better illustrated than in prayers of petition. The mystical word "abandonment" is much to be preferred to the more usual word "dependence" in this regard; for it indicates the movement outward and upward to God in which real prayer consists, rather than the inward, downward motion which all too often is mistaken for it. But another question is already taking shape. Just what does this creaturely recognition and opening have to do with the urgent importunity and beseeching prayer was called earlier? Is prayer a response or a request? As we follow up this question, it may be that a helpful light can be thrown on the rapport between prayer and God's providential reality.

I

There appears to be a paradox about prayer. The mystical interpretation, it seems, is quite at odds with the petitionary one. Some years ago the Abbé Poulain wrote a magnificent book, consisting mainly of an analysis of the types of inward or mental rather than vocal or written prayer. The author is trying to describe prayer from the inside, as it were, feeling for the place where words come from. He distinguishes two kinds, ordinary and extraordinary (or mystical). This is how he explains the difference between them:

Ordinary prayer may be compared to the atmosphere that surrounds our globe. The birds move about it at will. Thanks to its aid, they can rise above the earth, and they mount higher in proportion to the strength of their wing-beats. But this atmosphere has its limits. Above, lie those vast expanses that stretch away to the stars and beyond. Try as they may, they cannot penetrate thither, even by redoubling their own efforts. The eagle is as powerless as the rest. God alone can transport them to this region; were He to do so, they would lie passive in His hand, there would be no further need to use their wings. . . . This upper region, where the wing no longer has any power, is a figure of the mystic state. It resembles it also by its peace, its silence. Far from the turmoil of earth we enter into a space empty of all created things. God dwells there alone.[3]

Surely no one would wish to deny that this is a sublime view of the higher reaches of human prayer. And yet how stratospheric it is! Does it not moreover take us very far away from the position that prayer is petition, asking something of God? This book, instead, thinks of prayer as invocation, ecstatic transport, elevation. One is reminded of that very unorthodox mystic Simone Weil, who speaks in not dissimilar terms of "decreation," making oneself nothing before God, or of grace as making us "fall toward the heights." Or one may recall the advice given by F. W. Robertson, "Pray until prayer makes you cease to pray." According to this view it seems that whatever else prayer may be said to be, it is not petition. Any request made of God is not to be confused with that resting back and being carried which is truly prayer to God. The soul that is engaged in calling God's attention to itself is only dragging its feet. One must get off the ground of restive lack and need if one is even to begin praying. On such terms as these what more can we ask of God than he gives within the very experience of prayer itself? So prayer becomes not an act but rather a state, not beseeching but buoyancy, not inventory but inclusion in the space of God.

Yet how remote all this is from the sort of praying we know

[3] Augustin Poulain, *The Graces of Interior Prayer* (London: Kegan Paul, Trench, Trubner & Co., 1912), p. 2. Used by permission of B. Herder Book Co. and Routledge & Kegan Paul Ltd.

best! There are very few unscheduled mystical flights in the usual Sunday-morning church service, and we are not likely to belong in the ranks of those contemplatives and mystics upon whose reports the Abbé Poulain builds his whole case. Most pastors would be apt to believe that the more real prayer is to people, the closer to the ground of personal requirement and practical assistance it must come. Nor do the prayers of biblical prophets and apostles lend support to any such mystical interpretation; even the Lord's Prayer can hardly be fitted into it. We stand, it seems, within a humbler and more earthy kind of prayer tradition. The verbs of which we make use in our prayers are lamentably few—"give," "help," "lead," "pardon," "grant," or "bless"—but each of them represents a demand or claim made upon God, not the flight of the alone to the Alone. Must we not then fall back upon petition as the heart of prayer, after all?

Before we do so, however, let us consider another analogy given by Poulain, touching what he calls ordinary prayer. Think of an engineer and his locomotive. It rests with the man to start or stop the engine by turning the right lever. But all he does by this slight movement, says Poulain, is to bring an enormous power into play, that of steam under high pressure. This motive power dwells not in his own puny arm but in the steam, which nonetheless remains at his disposal. So the grace of God is like the steam, and man's praying is the turning of the lever that releases it.[4]

The analogy is certainly suggestive; man by his prayerful effort establishes a rapport with God's power, which is still prior and superior to his effort. By prayer we neither bend God's power to our own uses nor do we deflect God's purpose by the force of any technique. Precisely here, in fact, lies the whole great difference between prayer and magic. For despite much that is currently being said and written on the subject, prayer is not a technique for getting

[4] *Ibid.,* p. 1.

control of God. It is not prayer which moves the world but God, whose will and way are sought by means of praying. By his power we ourselves must be empowered if we are to do any good thing. The praying man or woman knows this and is acting on that knowledge.

This way of picturing prayer looks more clearly in the direction of Providence; the idea of concurrence or co-operation figures largely in it. But mechanical analogies can never convey the magnitude of this doctrine as it bears upon prayer. Thus the illustrations of radio and telephone communication, which have been employed *ad nauseam* in Christian pulpits of late, fall very far short of suggesting that prayer has the character of a truly providential, personal encounter. To the praying man or woman God is not a "party" or a "receiver"; as Hocking wrote, God does not occupy an "official position in my artificial world, . . . to be dealt with in polite and deadly distance." [5] No, on the contrary, the God of prayer is an eminently accessible and hearkening God. We pray to him just because we believe that he is ever more ready to hear than we to pray.

With this important proviso we may accept Poulain's analogy, for it makes two things about prayer helpfully clear. It indicates, as was said above, the priority and superiority of God with respect to our beseeching; and secondly, it stresses the possibility and the necessity of opening up communication with God through our own efforts. I shall speak of each of these points more fully, but here let it be noticed that it is the Christian belief in Providence, in God's sovereign concern, which enables us to bring and hold these truths together. Thus the apparent paradox in prayer becomes less formidable. We can say that if the *shape* of prayer is a request made of God, its *substance* is a response to him. Our asking is always in

[5] William Ernest Hocking, *The Meaning of God in Human Experience* (New Haven, Conn.: Yale University Press, 1912), p. 434.

addition a lifting up of what we ask for, an abandonment to Providence.

In petitionary prayer, for example, the urgency of desire or need is set within the recognition of a still more urgent Presence. The posture is that of supplication, yet the principle is that of opening ourselves to God's incoming influence and of exposing our concerns to his light and leading. Such prayer, the moment it becomes wheedling or ingratiating, ceases to be prayer.

Why then may not our response to God take shape as a request to him? That is clearly the most natural and normal way of acting out our reliance upon him who is, again in Edwards' words the "fountain of all good, from whom goodness flows as light from the sun." For if it is actually God to whom we are praying and not some shoddy idol made out of the whole cloth of human desire or need, then can any other mode of response be half so pertinent and right? One thing can certainly be said about petitionary prayer—it does not lend itself to any confusing of oneself with God, nor blur the distinction between creature and Creator. So long as you really want something from another, you know who he is and who you are, so that the very impulse of desire prevents you from changing places with him even in your thought or your imagination.

When we ask God for something, we do not become beggars or connivers or whiners but those who know in whom they have believed and from whom their help comes. Prayer is nothing without the living trust that what we need, God has to give us. It was Pindar, the poet of antiquity, who wrote, "Surely the great mind of Zeus pilots the destiny of those he loves." We Christians would alter the text, but our testimony would be the same. Because of Providence prayer is both response and request, and each insofar as it is the other. Our paradox turns out to be not so paradoxical, after all.

All this, however, leads directly into deeper truths concerning the "agreeableness" between prayer and Providence, to which we now turn.

II

There is a cherished passage in the New Testament which appears to be a kind of rule for praying: "Ask, and it will be given you; seek, and you will find; knock, and it will be opened to you. For every one who asks receives, and he who seeks finds, and to him who knocks it will be opened." (Matt. 7:7-8; also Luke 11:9-10.) If we could come to grips with the meaning of this passage, we should approach the center of an understanding of the providential impetus and import of our praying.

The words look simple and obvious enough on the surface. Doesn't this requirement-and-reward motif run all through Jesus' teachings? A condition is laid down; and when it is fulfilled, a satisfying consequence results. On this basis these words would mean something like the following: If you but ask, then you will get; if you want to find, you had better look; if you only knock, then it will be opened. That would put prayer on a sound, dependable footing, take a great deal of the risk out of it, and let one know just where he stood with God.

But how does it happen that this is not what Jesus says at all? His words lack entirely this "iffy," conditional character. He is not trying to put prayer on what can only be termed a paying basis. Although he says that it is ours to ask and God's to give, he does not issue any guarantee that what we ask for we shall get. These verses do not constitute in any sense a bargaining principle or contractual obligation.

The reason is that prayer itself may bring about not only the satisfaction but the actual correction of its dominant desire. I do not always come away from prayer with the same set of impulses that sent me into it. Having prayed the matter through, I may very possibly discover that my wishes have been changed, that my scheme of values has been rather surprisingly revalued. This, in fact, is a fairly common experience among praying people, though we would all agree that it is still not common enough. In the long run it is only prayer that can teach us what to pray for. Sooner or later we make Charlotte Brontë's prayer our own: "Grant us, O Lord, so to pray as to deserve to be heard." And then we learn that some prayers do not even deserve to be said.

That is why we must not take these cherished words of Jesus as meaning anything consequential and conditional. Emphatically, they do not suggest that prayer is a means of getting whatever we want from God as long as we make the right sort of adjustment to him. Nor do they guarantee that once we have done our part by asking, God must reply in kind and on the level of our asking.

Now, however, we must beware of understating our case. Jesus' words do set forth a definite, reliable rapport between prayer and Providence, even if in them the usual order of the *quid pro quo* is drastically reversed. Once the surface misunderstandings have been cleared up, there is still a positive equivalence between our asking and God's giving which needs to be thought through and declared. If a preacher was to give a sermon on this text, he would point out that it contains both a command and a promise but also that the promise comes before the command. The correlation between the two is not prudential but really providential. Our asking is in truth a "function" of God's giving, that is, the intended outcome of his providence.

This is how Augustine understood these words of Jesus:

He whom we desire to receive, causeth Himself to ask; He whom we wish to find causeth us to seek; He to whom we strive to attain causeth us to knock. . . . And when He is received, He brings it about

191

that He is besought by asking, by seeking, by knocking, to be more fully received.[6]

In prayer both God's ultimate otherness and his intimate nearness are given together. This makes each prayerful encounter with God at the same time an encouragement from God, as we are drawn, so to speak, into an elliptical orbit of responsiveness and invitation. The God who hears prayer is the same God who inspires it; and we should not be seeking him at all if we had not already found him —that is, had been found by him. At every step along the path of prayer a double search is taking place, both a human question divinely urged and a God-given answer humanly acknowledged.

Hence a praying man is not cannily sizing up his chances with God ahead of time, nor does he want to be sure that God will have the last word before he ventures to say the first. Something much more profound is involved—an elemental trust or credence that makes God, not self, the source and goal of every true prayer. For the fact that God hears prayer does not mean for a moment that he serves as our auxiliary or accomplice; what it means is that in God there is a readiness to give, to find, and to open which elicits ours to ask, to seek, and to knock. Perhaps the old word "condescension" taken in its original sense best catches up the priority, finality, and superiority of God to all prayer offered in his name. Prayer is itself the outcome of God's wish to help, his bending low to hear. The promise of Jesus disarms all our over-insistent, attention-getting devices, just as his command forbids all tête-à-tête with God.

Yet after all is said, this passage from the teachings of Jesus remains a comfortable word. It breathes not criticism and warning but a vastly heartening invitation. Assured of Providence, we venture boldly and eagerly to pray to God; and from this perspective prayer becomes in Karl Barth's phrase "a kind of breathing necessary

---

[6] *Enarrations on the Psalms,* CXVIII.

to life." To the Christian believer, aware that God is an available, anticipating God, there can never be any question whether to pray or not, since he cannot help praying.

Nevertheless we are commanded to pray. Why? By virtue of the fact that praying is ordained by Providence as the means whereby God has allowed his influence upon us to become a matter of our influencing him. Indeed, he has made of his mode of access to us our own mode of access to him. So he bestows on us not alone the good gifts which our prayer makes possible but the greater gift of prayer itself. In this way he allows us to answer him by asking, to be found of him by seeking. He encourages us to approach him freely, not in order to have proof of our devotion like some jealous suitor but for the purpose that his providence shall become operative and regnant in our own existence. Presumably he could accomplish this without any prayer from us, yet he chooses not to do so. This is because he desires us for himself, wants to be loved for his own sake, determines to be in very truth our Lord.

And notice that there are absolutely no strings attached to this command. Jesus does not oblige us with a handy list of preferred or forbidden items. He does not, for instance, prohibit praying for material benefits while extolling prayer for so-called spiritual blessings. As a matter of fact he has just told the disciples to pray for daily bread, which is about as material as anything that can be imagined. To restrict our praying in this manner not only would bound God in a quite unwarranted way; it would also be a much too simple method of maneuvering Providence to our own advantage. Jesus' words have to mean that we are to pray for anything we wish, anything we need. Let there be no limit to what we take to God in prayer, so that there may be no limit to God's reign and rule in all of life. It is far better to ask God for whatever we desire than to play God by deciding on our own what we ought to pray for. That would simply be pious magic all over again, wanting to control God by praying only for the right things in a way that is sure to get results. God himself will be the judge; ours is the task of putting everything up to him. Once more, Christian prayer is seen to be anchored in abandonment to Providence, that is, in our utter willingness to let God be God in all the issues of our life. As we have frequently had occasion to observe, that is the very core of faith. We must ask abundantly, since the measure of our asking shall be that of our receiving.

Furthermore, it is by obeying God's command that we accept his promise. When we pray, we do well, since we thereby present to God not only our desires and needs but the desiring, needy faith which is the prayer itself. And this faith voiced in prayer is an important new factor in the situation with which God is dealing; it is a benign and positive opportunity for God arising out of man's extremity. My need is great, my wish is strong; but God is good, is alone and utterly good. He may not give me what I ask, but he gives better gifts because I ask, since prayer is according to his purpose for human life. God wishes me to take him at his word, realizing that it is he who is the "Fountain of all good," "Good beyond all that is good," our "one chiefest eternal Good."

Yes, prayer stands or falls with Providence. One cannot honestly enter into it without viewing the whole of human existence as having worth and moment to God. What is more, its action matches its conception. For prayer begins by calling upon God and ends by resting the case with God. We address ourselves to one who reserves the right to grant or to withhold, one who in short remains God. This is every bit as true of thanksgiving as it is of supplication, or of praise as much as confession. Whenever we pray, we see our life as a divine appointing and directing. Our acts, if not our words, are pregnant with destiny. And thus it follows that the more prayer is in harmony with God's intention and initiative, the more it works together with his providence. Chrysostom was right: he who prays does have his hand on the rudder of the world. He has a creaturely share in bringing God's own purposes to pass. The eighteenth-century poet Christopher Smart put the matter well:

> Strong is the lion—like a coal
> His eye-ball—like a bastion's mole
> His chest against the foes:
>
> .   .   .   .
>
> But stronger still, in earth and air,
> And in the sea, the man of pray'r;
> And far beneath the tide;
> And in the seat to faith assign'd,
> Where ask is have, where seek is find,
> Where knock is open wide.[7]

Through and through, therefore, prayer is a providential enterprise, a way of man with God arising from and tending toward God's way with man. It is a living dialogue or it is nothing. It is even worse than nothing—an empty gesture, mocking and deriding those who use it. Yet when prayer achieves its true intent, it makes us, in the biblical sense, coworkers with God. Why pray? Because God wills it, occasions it, evokes it for the sake of having fellowship with us.

III

We Christians pray "through Jesus Christ our Lord." Because of him we have no hesitancy in praying but on the other hand a lively and constant hope that prayer will reap its God-appointed harvest. How and why does such a hope come about?

In and of itself prayer is a deed of hope; it means patiently waiting for the Lord. But how that hope is sharpened and made clear when prayers are consciously and deliberately offered in the

[7] *"A Song to David."*

name of Christ! For he is the reason why we *must* have hope. The world we live in has not yet accepted and followed him who is nevertheless its rightful Lord. He is still a stranger knocking at its gates. Have we not all erred and strayed from his ways like lost sheep? Have we not been staying too close to the devices—and the hopes—of our own hearts? Have we not once but many times, and all of us together, offended against his law of neighborly, forgiving love? We know full well the answer that must be given. Therefore we cannot be satisfied with even the most glorious missionary conquests, the dawning realization of our ecumenical dreams or the increasing size of our congregations. There is still too much to pray for and to work for. Christ is the reason why we must have hope.

But Christ is also the reason why we *can* have hope. Is he not the one in whom God bares his mighty arm and loving heart? Faith in him has brought release from man's primeval slavery to sin and fear and guilt. A new being, a new creation, in biblical terms, has been heralded by him, not merely glimpsed from afar. Indeed its foundations are already laid deep within the soil of historic fact. Therefore things can never be the same with us again. Through Christ we live in a time when all things are made new. Even the calendar knows that it is now A.D., not B.C. Prayer, more perhaps than any other Christian act, means self-commitment to the reign of God transcending, yet including, all the things of this world; it is what we do about the kingdom of God. It was shown earlier that petition really involves co-operation, and this makes all prayer worthy of the name an expectant sharing in the ultimate concerns of God. When offered in the spirit and truth which Christ brings, it begets in us a sure and lively hope.

Sometimes I think we make our hope in Jesus Christ more difficult and "dialectical" than it actually is. Our need to keep on hoping and the very reason why we have hope at all are grounded in the same great fact—that God discloses his holy, saving will by stepping down within the course of history to righten and align it. This is what we see taking place in Christ. When we call him our hope, we use such titles, borrowed from the Scriptures, as "author and finisher," "captain of [our] salvation," or "bright and morning star." By them all we declare that God is continuing to do through Christ that which he has begun in him, that what lies ahead is the consummation of that work, and that even now we are living in the new age which awaits its full and final realization.

Prayer, exactly like the Christian life as a whole, is therefore both anticipation and participation. A rather simple analogy may serve to make this clearer. It is a little like having a mortgage on your house. The bank holds the mortgage, but you actually own the house. As you have moved in and taken possession, you are legally accountable for what is your own property. It belongs to you really but not fully—yet. Every month you pay a bit more and reduce your debt to the bank. In the eyes of the law the house is as much yours now as it will be when all the debt is paid, but each payment now is an earnest of possession then. Without pushing this analogy so far that it becomes ludicrous instead of illuminating, may we not say that it shows how Christian hope is both a possession and a promise?

The man of faith and prayer is not simply marking time or looking ahead. He is entering here and now into the kingdom, the power, and the glory of the new creation. All that he does he does proleptically, that is, not so much toward the future as backward from the future, making his future goal his present motive. Language is notoriously difficult when it becomes a question of communicating this, but life abounds in instances of what it is and means. The earlier chapter on the mystery of time helps us to understand how such an "anticipated attainment" characterizes and defines all present effort, and the proper name for it is hope.

So Jesus Christ, who makes our hope possible, also makes it

necessary. He makes hope possible, for he is the very bodying forth of God's providential purpose, indeed God's very life bestowed in sovereign and holy concern for us. As we look back toward what God accomplished in him, we have every right to run with confident patience the race that is set before us. Yet it is also Christ who makes our hope necessary. His Kingdom tarries long; and although the stage is set for God's ultimate victory, the plot of history is thickening by the hour and must be played out to the finish. It is said of Arthur Hopkins, the theatrical producer, that he asked every playwright who submitted a manuscript to him, "How's your second act?" Well, we are living, working, praying, in God's second act. We know how things are coming out in the end, but we are not there yet. To hope therefore in Christ is both our right and our duty.

Praying is hoping, even when it is a hoping against hope. There is a fine and sensitive balance which has to be maintained where hope in Jesus Christ is concerned. We must never put so much stress upon the final victory that we blind ourselves to the power of the new creation working in us now above all that we can ask or think. Yet neither should we pin our hopes upon God's redeeming work disclosed at one point *in* history to the extent that we neglect God's providential ordering *of* history as revealing his design for our salvation. Prayer lives and moves and has its being, as it were, between these limits or poles.

When we Christians think about the end of history, we have in mind two truths which are not contradictory but complementary to each other. First, "end" means "goal." God is bringing to pass within the structures of time and space and human freedom the purpose for which he created the world. We do not have to wait for this to happen, since it happens every moment. In God's sight history is a making good. Not all events and certainly not all human beings are the knowing, willing agents of God's purpose; but all are his perhaps unwitting instruments. Thus in the words of John Oman:

> By no setting of our hearts on wickedness or doing evil with both hands can we prevent God from using us. Our folly will serve Him when our wisdom fails; our wrath praise Him, though our wills rebel. Yet, as God's instruments without intention and in our own despite, we generally serve God's ends only as we defeat our own.

But, he continues,

> To be God's agent is quite another matter. This we are only as we learn God's will, respond to His call, work faithfully together with Him, and find our highest ends in fulfilling His.[8]

Whether we are instruments only or also agents, it remains true that history moves toward its fulfillment slowly, often secretly, but always surely. There is room in Christian hope, then, for a sturdy, workmanlike confidence in genuine improvement and real progress on our own part, corresponding to our confidence that God is working his purpose out upon the larger stage. And prayer represents our willing self-conforming to this vaster purpose; in biblical phrase it is our venturing boldly into the throne room of the Most High.

Secondly, "end" means "finish." When God's will is done on earth as it is done in heaven, history will be over and concluded; it will have served its purpose. Some earnest fellow Christians see this finality in terms of naïve imaginings and literal time schedules; they want to make the end of history a predictable and even historical fact. Although these apocalyptic fancies cannot be accepted as possessing in themselves historical truth, they nevertheless contain a precious kernel of truth about history. Belief in the second coming

---

[8] *The Paradox of the World* (New York: The Macmillan Co.), p. 30.

and the last judgment means that he who dwells with us as our present, risen Lord is by the same token the approaching Lord. If Christ comes once, he is forever coming; he is the coming Son of man. Of old he came "all so still, to his mother's bower." He comes continually into hearts that prepare him room. And he will come again to judge in glory both the quick and the dead. That will mean that God is done with history; the "end time" will have come. And whatever God may plan regarding other worlds or other aeons than our own, he will have called it a day so far as this world and its history are concerned.

Prayer is the habit of the soul that is entirely suited to our situation of living "between the times." Thus we are kept humble and expectant even as we are encouraged and assured, so long as prayer is rooted deeply in what God has done, is doing, and will do for man, from Eden to the New Jerusalem and all the way between.

Again, prayer in the name of Jesus Christ is our own rendezvous with destiny, the Christian word for which is "Providence." It has not been left wholly to ourselves what we shall make of our life, but rather we are God's coworkers in the shaping of it. Therefore what we do and plan is embraced within a vaster action and intention—a mysterious work and will in which we are included. So we believe; so also we pray.

In Christ our personal histories are merged, bound up, with world history. Because he has revealed to us the heart of things, we can give ourselves into the keeping of the whole of things. That which is probably the central mystery of Providence, made everlastingly plain in Jesus, is the way in which the God whom he called Father, who is no respecter of persons, yet cares for each human being as if he alone mattered. So while no one may claim to be God's "only child," everyone may lift his heart to God in prayerful trust. There is food for thought, I think, in the reply of Galileo to the people who accused him of moving God too far out of the universe so that men felt neglected and forsaken. "The sun," he answered, "which has all those planets revolving around it and dependent on it for their orderly functions, can ripen a bunch of grapes as if it had nothing else in the world to do." So too in Christian faith expressed through prayer, Providence is always both individual and universal, since it means the structuring of God's sovereign concern for each and every creature.

Why should we consent to believe this? Is there not abundant evidence to the contrary? That is certainly true, and we do not need to repeat the tiresome catalogue of human misery and perversity in order to learn just how true it is. The real question, however, which we have been facing in these chapters is whether that is the whole and only truth. We Christians say that it is not. We dare to believe that God is keeping faith with us, standing by us, overshadowing us, and leading us in ways past finding out all through our earthly journeying.

It is as if through the babel of conflicting voices a Word could still be heard saying, "Fear not!" It is as if amidst the crisscrossed claims and pressures making up the tangled skein of destiny in history, a thread of meaning—broken sometimes but always being taken up again—gave a kind of homespun beauty to our life together. Or it is as if, beyond our darkness and forcing its way into it, a Presence were materializing, making itself felt, the mighty love of him whom the darkness cannot hide because to him darkness and light are both alike.

The name of the Word that insists upon being heard, this meaning which we are permitted to detect and piece out, this Presence taking quiet, solid shape, is Jesus Christ. In him all things cohere, hang together, make real sense. According to his own good pleasure and in his own good time, God comes to seek and to save those who are lost.

For in Christ world history becomes sacred, saving history. The rise and fall of empires, the interminable struggling for advantage, the development of science and technics, the panorama of philosophies and religions, are all summed up and reckoned in him. And hence through faith in him we are emboldened to believe that God can turn to good the worst that history can show. No power of fate, no peril of freedom, no threat of time or the tragic or technical self-degradation, is able to separate us from God's love made plain in him. In Christ, God has given us a way that is forever open, a door into his providence.

It is prayer that knocks upon that door, but it is the prayer-hearing God who comes through it. In common with all Christian believers through the ages, Benedict knew that and so cried out with joy: "Behold, the Lord in His goodness shows us Himself the way of life!"

INDEX